WebGL: Up and Running

Tony Parisi

O'REILLY®

Beijing · Cambridge · Farnham · Köln · Sebastopol · Tokyo

WebGL: Up and Running

by Tony Parisi

Copyright © 2012 Tony Parisi. All rights reserved.

Printed in the United States of America.

Published by O'Reilly Media, Inc., 1005 Gravenstein Highway North, Sebastopol, CA 95472.

O'Reilly books may be purchased for educational, business, or sales promotional use. Online editions are also available for most titles (*http://my.safaribooksonline.com*). For more information, contact our corporate/institutional sales department: 800-998-9938 or *corporate@oreilly.com*.

Editor: Mary Treseler	**Proofreader:** Jasmine Kwityn
Production Editor: Iris Febres	**Indexer:** Jay Marchand
Copyeditor: Audrey Doyle	**Cover Designer:** Karen Montgomery
	Interior Designer: David Futato
	Illustrators: Robert Romano and Rebecca Demarest

August 2012:   First Edition

Revision History for the First Edition:

2012-08-02   First release

See *http://oreilly.com/catalog/errata.csp?isbn=9781449323578* for release details.

ISBN: 978-1-449-32357-8

[LSI]

Table of Contents

Foreword

In the summer of 1996, I had the privilege of doing a summer internship in the Cosmo Software division of Silicon Graphics, Inc., which was developing a Virtual Reality Markup Language (VRML) player for web browsers. VRML brought interactive 3D graphics to the World Wide Web for the first time. The Web was young, and it was exciting to see 3D integrated into the experience at such an early stage.

VRML unfortunately didn't gain the broad adoption its supporters had hoped for. From a purely technical standpoint, there were two contributing factors. First, the programmability was limited due to poor performance at the time of the available scripting languages' virtual machines. This meant that it wasn't possible to write general-purpose code that affected the 3D scene, inherently limiting the domains to which VRML could be applied. Second, the rendering model was based on the original OpenGL API's fixed function graphics pipeline. This meant it was not possible to add new kinds of visual effects beyond those that had been designed into the system.

In the intervening 16 years, there have been dramatic advancements in graphics technologies and computer language implementations. The 3D graphics pipeline has become fully programmable, meaning that artists and designers can create lighting and shading effects limited only by their imaginations. Additionally, huge performance increases in the virtual machines for programming languages like JavaScript make it possible to change every aspect of the 3D scene, all the way down to the individual vertices of the component triangles, in every frame. This flexibility makes it possible to write arbitrary 3D applications directly in the web browser for the first time.

The WebGL API builds on decades of computer graphics work and research that culminated some years ago in the development of the OpenGL ES 2.0 API, a small, purely shader-based graphics library that ships in nearly every new smartphone and mobile device. The WebGL working group and community are hopeful that exposing the power of the 3D graphics processor to the Web in a safe and robust manner will yield a long-anticipated wave of new and exciting 3D web applications that run on every operating system and on every kind of computing device.

Tony has written an accessible yet comprehensive book that covers a wide range of practical techniques for the development of 3D applications on the Web. His book will help the novice get up and running, but also contains enough advanced information that even the 3D graphics expert will learn something new. Tony rapidly moves past the basics of displaying 3D meshes, and presents interesting, useful material on topics including visual effects, animation, interaction, and content creation, culminating in the development of a working prototype of a 3D game. It's a good read; I enjoyed it and hope that you will, too.

—Ken Russell
Chair, WebGL Working Group, the Khronos Group

Preface

In early 1994, Tim Berners-Lee put out an open call for a virtual reality specification for the Web; Mark Pesce and I answered. Only being able to afford one plane ticket, we sent Mark to Geneva to present our *Labyrinth* prototype at the first-ever World Wide Web Developers' Conference. With typical bombast, Mark announced to the packed room that we had "already done it." Our demo was simple but to the point: a rotating 3D object in a window that, when clicked, launched a web browser and navigated to a hyperlink. Within a few weeks, we had a mailing list, and Virtual Reality Markup Language (VRML), the seminal effort to put 3D on the Web, was underway.

A decade and a half later, 3D had finally made it into the browser, though it wouldn't be in the form that Mark and I imagined. VRML was well intentioned but far too early— before broadband connections and dedicated graphics hardware were mainstream. VRML inspired successors and copycats, but those too fell by the wayside. Technologies came and went as people continued to hammer away at the problem. Finally, around 2009, we reached the turning point: the industry rallied around a new standard called WebGL. It's 2012 now, and it appears that WebGL is here to stay.

WebGL brings 3D to the browser, providing a JavaScript interface to the graphics hardware on your machine. Based on OpenGL ES (the same graphics running in your smartphone and tablet), it is developed and supported by the makers of major desktop and mobile web browsers. With WebGL, any programmer can create stunning graphics that reach millions of users via the Web: no-download games, big data visualizations, product displays, training simulations…the list goes on.

While there are dozens of online resources devoted to WebGL, and many libraries and tools now supporting it, the information is scattered, and the coverage incomplete. The WebGL API is really low-level—likely out of reach for the typical developer—and in its raw form accessible only to experienced 3D programmers. But the premise and promise of WebGL is to make 3D available to everyone: any consumer with modern hardware and a recent browser, any developer with a text editor and some imagination. We need a way to bridge the gap between the incredible power now at our disposal, and the knowledge and tools to put it into practice.

That's why I wrote this book.

Audience

If you're a web programmer or designer, this book will get you up and running with WebGL. The book assumes you have HTML, CSS, and JavaScript experience, and familiarity with jQuery and Ajax. But that's about it. You don't need 3D graphics experience—there's a brief tutorial in Chapter 1 to show you the fundamentals—and you don't need to be an expert game developer.

How This Book Is Organized

The book consists of eight chapters divided among three major parts, plus an appendix:

- Chapters 1 and 2 provide an overview of the WebGL API and Three.js, the open source JavaScript library used for the programming examples.

- Chapters 3 through 6 dive into the details of programming graphics, animation, and interaction, and explore WebGL's breakthrough capabilities for integrating 2D and 3D into a seamless user experience.

- Chapters 7 and 8 cover real-world WebGL production topics, from authoring tools and file formats to building robust and secure WebGL applications. In Chapter 8 we build our first full application, a car racing game.

- Appendix A lists resources for learning more about WebGL development, the WebGL standard, and related technologies and tools.

Most of the chapters follow a pattern: explain a concept, dive into some code to illustrate it, and pop back up again for a look around before moving on to the next idea. Occasionally I take a side trip to discuss issues near and dear to my heart, or go on a brief rant about some best practice or other. I hope I have struck the right balance between teaching and preaching; feel free to let me know how I have done on that score.

If you get stuck on any of the example code, let it wash over you and come back to it later. You can almost always read the concept sections as a whole piece and come back to the code when you're ready. And don't hesitate to open up the examples in your favorite WebGL-enabled browser and walk through them in the debugger; that's usually the best way to learn.

The majority of the examples use a toolkit called Three.js, an excellent open source engine built on top of WebGL. Early on, I had to make a choice about whether to bombard you, the reader, with the many low-level details of the WebGL API—a wonderfully flexible, superbly powerful, but decidedly user-unfriendly drawing system—or instead provide the basic information you need to start building applications quickly. The choice was abundantly clear: get you up and running fast. If you like how it's going and want to know more about what's under the WebGL hood, there are plenty of resources for that. We have listed some of those in Appendix A.

The developers of WebGL have created something unique and amazing: 3D running in the browser, blending seamlessly with other information on the page, mashed up with data from anywhere in the world, represents an unlimited palette for you to build whatever you can imagine. This is more than the sum of its parts; it's a new medium and a whole new ball game. WebGL programming may not come easy at first, but I promise that if you make the effort, an exciting new world awaits.

Conventions Used in This Book

The following typographical conventions are used in this book:

Italic
: Indicates new terms, URLs, email addresses, filenames, and file extensions

`Constant width`
: Used for program listings, as well as within paragraphs to refer to program elements such as variable or function names, databases, data types, environment variables, statements, and keywords

`Constant width bold`
: Shows commands or other text that should be typed literally by the user

`Constant width italic`
: Shows text that should be replaced with user-supplied values or by values determined by context

 This icon signifies a tip, suggestion, or general note.

This Book's Example Files

You can download all of the code examples for this book from GitHub at the following location:

https://github.com/tparisi/WebGLBook

In the example files, you will find the completed versions of the applications built in the book, which will contain all the code required to run them. In a few cases, you will need to download additional content files, such as 3D models, from their original sites before running the application; consult the README file in the top-level folder for details.

Using Code Examples

This book is here to help you get your job done. In general, you may use the code in this book in your programs and documentation. You do not need to contact us for permission unless you're reproducing a significant portion of the code. For example, writing a program that uses several chunks of code from this book does not require permission. Selling or distributing a CD-ROM of examples from O'Reilly books does require permission. Answering a question by citing this book and quoting example code does not require permission. Incorporating a significant amount of example code from this book into your product's documentation does require permission.

We appreciate, but do not require, attribution. An attribution usually includes the title, author, publisher, and ISBN. For example: "*WebGL: Up and Running* by Tony Parisi (O'Reilly). Copyright 2012 Tony Parisi, 978-1-449-32357-8."

If you feel your use of code examples falls outside fair use or the permission given here, feel free to contact us at *permissions@oreilly.com*.

Safari® Books Online

Safari Books Online (*http://my.safaribooksonline.com*) is an on-demand digital library that delivers expert content in both book and video form from the world's leading authors in technology and business. Technology professionals, software developers, web designers, and business and creative professionals use Safari Books Online as their primary resource for research, problem solving, learning, and certification training.

Safari Books Online offers a range of product mixes and pricing programs for organizations, government agencies, and individuals. Subscribers have access to thousands of books, training videos, and prepublication manuscripts in one fully searchable database from publishers like O'Reilly Media, Prentice Hall Professional, Addison-Wesley Professional, Microsoft Press, Sams, Que, Peachpit Press, Focal Press, Cisco Press, John Wiley & Sons, Syngress, Morgan Kaufmann, IBM Redbooks, Packt, Adobe Press, FT Press, Apress, Manning, New Riders, McGraw-Hill, Jones & Bartlett, Course Technology, and dozens more. For more information about Safari Books Online, please visit us online.

How to Contact Us

Please address comments and questions concerning this book to the publisher:

O'Reilly Media, Inc.
1005 Gravenstein Highway North
Sebastopol, CA 95472
800-998-9938 (in the United States or Canada)
707-829-0515 (international or local)
707-829-0104 (fax)

We have a web page for this book, where we list errata, examples, and any additional information. You can access this page at *http://oreil.ly/WebGL_UR*.

To comment or ask technical questions about this book, send email to: *bookquestions@oreilly.com*.

For more information about our books, courses, conferences, and news, see our website at *http://www.oreilly.com*.

Find us on Facebook: *http://facebook.com/oreilly*

Follow us on Twitter: *http://twitter.com/oreillymedia*

Watch us on YouTube: *http://www.youtube.com/oreillymedia*

Acknowledgments

Like WebGL itself, this book is the result of a collaborative effort and would not exist without the help and support of many great people. First, I would like to thank the team at O'Reilly, starting with my editor, Mary Treseler. Books on a new technology are always risky; regardless, Mary went full speed ahead to make this title happen. Her thoughtfulness about the subject matter and constant encouragement for a first-time author were much appreciated. The editorial, production, and marketing staff at O'Reilly, too numerous to mention here, were stellar and helped make writing the book a wonderful experience for me.

I am extremely grateful for the top-notch technical reviews done by Giles Thomas (of *Learning WebGL* fame), Mike Korcynski, Ray Camden, and Raffaele Cecco. Their detailed comments kept me honest on terminology and helped clarify the examples. Most importantly, their positive feedback on the early chapters gave me a much-needed moral boost when the writing got tough.

A lot of 3D content goes into crafting a graphically oriented programming book. I would like to thank the many artists who granted me permission to redistribute their work with the book samples. You can find detailed art credits in the README as well as the HTML and JavaScript files that go with each example. I would like to give special thanks to Christell Gause, head of support at TurboSquid, for his diligent efforts in helping me obtain permission from the many TurboSquid artists whose content is featured here. Also, I could not have created the examples for this book without additional help and/or contributed content from data junkie Theo Armour, 3D programming ace Don Olmstead, and 3D artist Arefin Mohiuddin of Sunglass.io.

WebGL is blessed to have a strong community of developers. I would like to thank the three.js developers, including guru Ricardo Cabello ("Mr.doob") and contributors Branislav Ulicny ("AlteredQualia") and Tim Knip, for their patience with my often-naïve questions and their overall enthusiasm for the project. I owe an eternal debt of gratitude to Ken Russell, the WebGL working group chair and WebGL development lead at Google. Ken has not only built a great product, but he kindly agreed to write the foreword for this book.

Finally, I would like to thank my friends and family. Mark Pesce, my old VRML partner in crime, is a veteran author. His commitment to excellence in writing and his passion for emerging technology have been a constant source of inspiration to me over the years. Many thanks to my buddy and sometimes-business-partner Scott Foe, who was always supportive of this book, despite the major distraction it created from our day-to-day startup. Last but not least, my family provided the moral support, patience, and loving environment that any author needs to thrive. More than that, they pitched in on the logistics: my 10-year-old, Lucian, gets props for play-testing most of the examples in the book, and my wife, Marina, kept me honest with art direction so that my cobbled-together examples would at least have a consistent look and coherent story.

CHAPTER 1

An Introduction to WebGL

An interactive live jellyfish forest, with hundreds of jellies pulsating and rays of sunlight streaming from the surface of the sea to the murky depths below—under your control. A networked virtual reality simulation of the human body, including the skeletal, circulatory, and other major systems: with your mouse you can peel back the layers of the body, drop pins on interesting parts for future reference, and share a hyperlink with colleagues and students. An immersive massively multiplayer universe, filled with your Twitter friends and followers. No, you haven't accidentally channel-flipped to an episode of PBS's *Nova*, and you're not watching a trailer for the latest Ridley Scott film. This stuff of the future is running in your web browser—right now. It's called WebGL.

Figure 1-1. WebGL jellyfish simulation (http://chrysaora.com/), reproduced with permission from Aleksander Rodic

WebGL is the new standard for 3D graphics on the Web. With WebGL, developers can harness the full power of the computer's graphics rendering hardware using only JavaScript, a web browser, and a standard web technology stack. Before WebGL, developers had to rely on plug-ins or native applications and ask their users to download and install custom software in order to deliver a true 3D experience.

WebGL is part of the HTML5 family of technologies. While not in the official specification, it is shipped with most browsers that support HTML5. Like Web Workers, Web Sockets, and other technologies outside the official W3C recommendations, WebGL is an essential component in an emerging suite that is transforming the modern browser into a first-class application platform.

WebGL works on the majority of desktops, as well as a growing number of mobile browsers. There are millions of WebGL-enabled seats already installed, most likely including the machines you run at home and in your office. WebGL is at the center of a vibrant and growing ecosystem that is making the web experience more visually rich and engaging. There are hundreds of sites, applications, and tools being developed, with applications ranging from games to data visualization, computer-aided design, and consumer retail.

While the low-level nature of the WebGL API may appear daunting at first, there are several open source JavaScript toolkits that take the grunt work out of development. I want to be careful not to oversell this—3D is still hard work—but these tools at least make it possible for mere mortals with modest web development experience to get into the WebGL business. So maybe it's finally time for you to create that hit game you always wanted to make. Or maybe today is the day when you blow your boss's mind with a dazzling intro graphic for your home page.

In this chapter, we will take a quick tour of the low-level underpinnings of WebGL to give you a foundation. For the majority of the book, we will use a high-level 3D toolkit, Three.js, which hides many of the messy details. But it is important to know what these tools are built upon, so let's start by exploring WebGL's core concepts and API.

WebGL—A Technical Definition

WebGL is developed and maintained by the Khronos Group, the standards body that also governs OpenGL, COLLADA, and other specifications you may have heard of. Here is the official description of WebGL, from the Khronos website:

> WebGL is a royalty-free, cross-platform API that brings OpenGL ES 2.0 to the web as a 3D drawing context within HTML, exposed as low-level Document Object Model interfaces. It uses the OpenGL shading language, GLSL ES, and can be cleanly combined with other web content that is layered on top or underneath the 3D content. It is ideally suited for dynamic 3D web applications in the JavaScript programming language, and will be fully integrated in leading web browsers.

This definition comprises several core ideas. Let's deconstruct them here:

WebGL is an API

WebGL is accessed exclusively through a set of JavaScript programming interfaces; there are no accompanying tags like there are with HTML. 3D rendering in WebGL is analogous to 2D drawing using the `Canvas` element, in that it is all done through JavaScript API calls. In fact, access to WebGL is provided using the existing `Canvas` element and obtaining a special drawing context specific to WebGL.

WebGL is based on OpenGL ES 2.0

OpenGL ES is an adaption of the long-established 3D rendering standard OpenGL. The "ES" stands for "embedded systems," meaning that it has been tailored for use in small computing devices, most notably phones and tablets. OpenGL ES is the API that powers 3D graphics for the iPhone, the iPad, and Android phones and tablets. . WebGL's designers felt that, by basing the API on OpenGL ES's small footprint, delivering a consistent, cross-platform, cross-browser 3D API for the Web would be more achievable.

WebGL combines with other web content

WebGL layers on top of or underneath other page content. The 3D canvas can take up just a portion of the page, or the whole page. It can reside inside `<div>` tags that are z-ordered. This means that you develop your 3D graphics using WebGL, but all your other elements are built using familiar old HTML. The browser composites (combines) all of the graphics on the page into a seamless experience for the user.

WebGL is built for dynamic web applications

WebGL has been designed with web delivery in mind. WebGL starts with OpenGL ES, but it has been adapted with specific features that integrate well with web browsers, work with the JavaScript language, and are friendly for web delivery.

WebGL is cross-platform

WebGL is capable of running on any operating system, on devices ranging from phones and tablets to desktop computers.

WebGL is royalty-free

Like all open web specifications, WebGL is free to use. Nobody will be asking you to pay royalties for the privilege.

The makers of Chrome, Firefox, Safari, and Opera have committed significant resources to developing and supporting WebGL, and engineers from these teams are also key members of the working group that develops the specification. The WebGL specification process is open to all Khronos members, and there are also mailing lists open to the public. See Appendix A for mailing list information and other specification resources.

3D Graphics—A Primer

"Math is hard!"

—Barbie

As sexist as the infamous quote may be, I have to say that whenever I code something in 3D, I, like Barbie, get a very strong urge to indulge in shop therapy. It's hard stuff and it often involves more than a little math. Luckily, you won't have to be a math whiz to build something in WebGL; we are going to use libraries that do most of the hard work for us. But it is important to understand what's going on under the hood, and to that end, here is my attempt to summarize the entire discipline of interactive 3D graphics in a few pages.

3D Coordinate Systems

3D drawing takes place, not surprisingly, in a 3D coordinate system. Anyone familiar with 2D Cartesian coordinate systems such as you find on graph paper, or in the window coordinates of an HTML document, knows about x and y values. These 2D coordinates define where `<div>` tags are located on a page, or where the virtual "pen" or "brush" draws in the case of the HTML `Canvas` element. Similarly, 3D drawing takes place in a 3D coordinate system, where there is an additional coordinate, z, which describes depth (i.e., how far into or out of the screen an object is drawn). The WebGL coordinate system is arranged as depicted in Figure 1-2, with x running horizontally left to right, y running vertically bottom to top, and positive z coming out of the screen.

If you are already comfortable with the concept of the 2D coordinate system, I think the transition to a 3D coordinate system is pretty straightforward. However, from here on, things get a little complicated.

Meshes, Polygons, and Vertices

While there are several ways to draw 3D graphics, by far the most common is to use a *mesh*. A mesh is an object composed of one or more polygonal shapes, constructed out of *vertices* (x, y, z triples) defining coordinate positions in 3D space. The polygons most typically used in meshes are triangles (groups of three vertices) and quads (groups of four vertices). 3D meshes are often referred to as *models*.

Figure 1-3 illustrates a 3D mesh. The dark lines outline the quads that comprise the mesh, defining the shape of the face. (You would not see these lines in the final rendered image; they are included for reference.) The x, y, and z components of the mesh's vertices define the shape *only*; surface properties of the mesh, such as the color and shading, are defined using additional attributes, as we will discuss shortly.

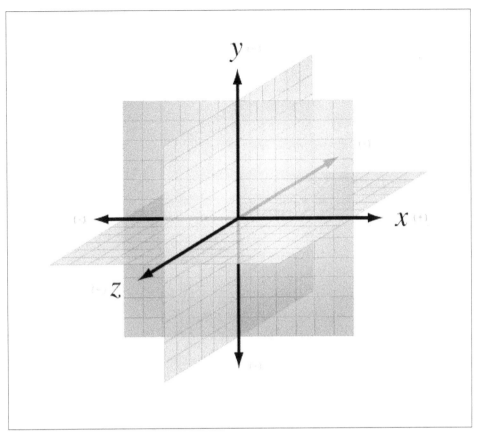

Figure 1-2. A 3D coordinate system (https://commons.wikimedia.org/wiki/File: 3D_coordinate_system.svg; Creative Commons Attribution-Share Alike 3.0 Unported license)

Materials, Textures, and Lights

The surface of a mesh is defined using additional attributes beyond the *x*, *y*, and *z* vertex positions. Surface attributes can be as simple as a single solid color, or they can be complex, comprising several pieces of information that define, for example, how light reflects off the object or how shiny the object looks. Surface information can also be represented using one or more bitmaps, known as *texture maps* (or simply *textures*). Textures can define the literal surface look (such as an image printed on a t-shirt), or they can be combined with other textures to achieve sophisticated effects such as bumpiness or iridescence. In most graphics systems, the surface properties of a mesh are referred to collectively as *materials*. Materials typically rely on the presence of one or more *lights*, which (as you may have guessed) define how a scene is illuminated.

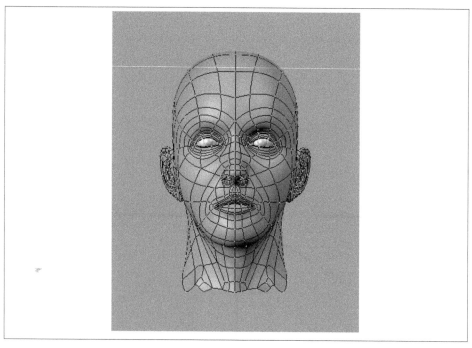

Figure 1-3. A 3D mesh (http://upload.wikimedia.org/wikipedia/commons/8/88/ Blender3D_UVTexTut1.png; Creative Commons Attribution-Share Alike 3.0 Unported license)

The head in Figure 1-3 has a material with a purple color and shading defined by a light source emanating from the left of the model (note the shadows on the right side of the face).

Transforms and Matrices

3D meshes are defined by the positions of their vertices. It would get awfully tedious to change a mesh's vertex positions every time you want to move it to a different part of the view, especially if the mesh were continually moving across the screen or otherwise animating. For this reason, most 3D systems support *transforms*, operations that move the mesh by a relative amount without having to loop through every vertex, explicitly changing its position. Transforms allow a rendered mesh to be scaled, rotated, and translated (moved) around, without actually changing any values in its vertices.

A transform is typically represented by a *matrix*, a mathematical object containing an array of values used to compute the transformed positions of vertices. If you are a linear algebra geek like me, you probably feel comfortable with this idea. If not, please don't break into a cold sweat. The Three.js toolkit we are using in this book lets us treat matrices like black boxes: we just say translate, rotate, or scale and the right thing happens.

Cameras, Perspective, Viewports, and Projections

Every rendered scene requires a point of view from which the user will be viewing it. 3D systems typically use a *camera*, an object that defines where (relative to the scene) the user is positioned and oriented, as well as other real-world camera properties such as the size of the field of view, which defines *perspective* (i.e., objects farther away appearing smaller). The camera's properties combine to deliver the final rendered image of a 3D scene into a 2D *viewport* defined by the window or canvas.

Cameras are almost always represented using a couple of matrices. The first matrix defines the position and orientation of the camera, much like the matrix used for transforms (see the earlier discussion). The second matrix is a specialized one that represents the translation from the 3D coordinates of the camera into the 2D drawing space of the viewport. It is called the *projection matrix*. I know—sigh—there's that pesky math again! But the details of camera matrices are nicely hidden in most toolkits, so you usually can just point, shoot, and render.

Figure 1-4 depicts the core concepts of the camera, viewport, and projection. At the lower left, we see an icon of an eye; this represents the location of the camera. The red vector pointing to the right (in this diagram labeled as the x-axis) represents the direction in which the camera is pointing. The blue cubes are the objects in the 3D scene. The green and red rectangles are, respectively, the *near* and *far clipping planes*. These two planes define the boundaries of a subset of the 3D space, known as the *view volume* or *view frustum*. Only objects within the view volume are actually rendered to the screen. The near clipping plane is equivalent to the viewport, where we will see the final rendered image.

Cameras are extremely powerful, as they ultimately define the viewer's relationship to a 3D scene and provide a sense of realism. They also provide another weapon in the animator's arsenal: by dynamically moving the camera around, you can create cinematic effects and control the narrative experience.

Shaders

There is one last topic before we conclude our exploration of 3D graphics: shaders. In order to render the final image for a mesh, a developer must define exactly how vertices, transforms, materials, lights, and the camera interact with one another to create that image. This is done using shaders. A *shader* (also known as a *programmable shader*) is a chunk of program code that implements algorithms to get the pixels for a mesh onto

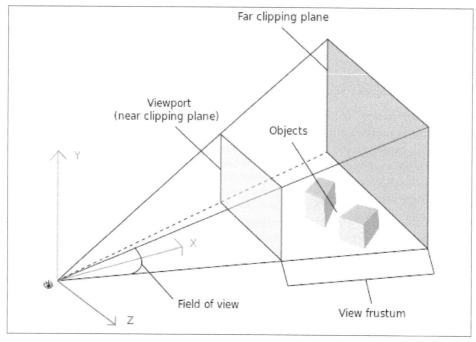

Figure 1-4. Camera, viewport, and projection (http://obviam.net/index.php/3d-programming-with-android-projections-perspective/), reproduced with permission

the screen. Shaders are typically defined in a high-level C-like language and compiled into code usable by the graphics processing unit (GPU). Most modern computers come equipped with a GPU, a processor separate from the CPU that is dedicated to rendering 3D graphics.

If you read my earlier decoded definition of WebGL carefully, you may have noticed that I glossed over one bit. From the official Khronos description:

> …It uses the OpenGL shading language, GLSL ES…

Unlike many graphics systems, where shaders are an optional and/or advanced feature, WebGL *requires* shaders. You heard me right: when you program in WebGL, you *must* define shaders or your graphics won't show up on the screen. WebGL implementations assume the presence of a GPU. The GPU understands vertices, textures, and little else; it has no concept of material, light, or transform. The translation between those high-level inputs and what the GPU puts on the screen is done by the shader, and the shader is created by the developer.

So now you know why I didn't bring up this topic earlier: I didn't want to scare you! Shader programming can be pretty intimidating, and writing a C-like program, short though it may be, seems like an awfully high price to pay just to get an image on the screen. However, take heart: many popular libraries written for WebGL come with prebuilt shaders that you can just drop into your code and are powerful enough to cover all your conceivable shading needs.

 I should note here that shaders aren't only about pain and suffering. They exist for a very good reason. Shaders give the graphics program-mer full control over every vertex and pixel that gets rendered. This power can be used to create the most awesome effects, from uncanny photorealism (such as the jellyfish in Figure 1-1) to cartoonish fantasy. But with this great power also comes great responsibility. Shaders are an advanced topic, and I don't want to climb that mountain together unless we have a thorough understanding of the basics. That's why the examples in this book will stick to using simple shaders.

The WebGL API

The basic concepts of interactive graphics haven't changed much over the past several years. Implementations, however, are continually evolving, especially due to the recent proliferation of devices and operating systems. Bedrock among these changing tides has been OpenGL. Originally developed in the late 1980s, OpenGL has been an industry-standard API for a very long time, having endured competitive threats from Microsoft DirectX to emerge as the undisputed standard for programming 3D graphics.

But not all OpenGLs are the same. The characteristics of various platforms, including desktop computers, set-top televisions, smartphones, and tablets, are so divergent that different editions of OpenGL had to be developed. OpenGL ES (for "embedded sys-tems") is the version of OpenGL developed to run on small devices such as set-top TVs and smartphones. Perhaps unforeseen at the time of its development, it turns out that OpenGL ES forms the ideal core for WebGL. It is small and lean, which means that not only is it (relatively) straightforward to implement in a browser, but it makes it much more likely that the developers of the different browsers implement it consistently, and that a WebGL application written for one browser will work identically in another browser.

All of this high-performance, portable goodness comes with a downside. The lean nature of WebGL puts the onus on application developers to layer on top of it their own object models, scene graphs, display lists, and other structures that many veteran graphics programmers have come to take for granted. Of more concern is that, to the average web developer, WebGL represents a steep learning curve full of truly alien concepts. The good news here is that there are several open source code libraries out there that make

WebGL development quite approachable, and even fun. Think of them as existing at the level of jQuery or Prototype.js, though the analogy is rough at best. We will be talking about one such library, Three.js, in just a few short pages. But before we get to that, we are going to take a quick tour of the underpinnings, the drive train if you will, of WebGL.

The Anatomy of a WebGL Application

At the end of the day, WebGL is just a drawing library—a drawing library on steroids, granted, considering that the graphics you can draw with WebGL are truly awe-inspiring and take full advantage of the powerful GPU hardware on most machines today. But it is really just another kind of canvas, akin to the 2D Canvas supported in all HTML5 browsers. In fact, WebGL actually uses the HTML5 `<canvas>` element to get 3D graphics into the browser page.

In order to render WebGL into a page, an application must, at a minimum, perform the following steps:

1. Create a canvas element.
2. Obtain a drawing context for the canvas.
3. Initialize the viewport.
4. Create one or more buffers containing the data to be rendered (typically vertices).
5. Create one or more matrices to define the transformation from vertex buffers to screen space.
6. Create one or more shaders to implement the drawing algorithm.
7. Initialize the shaders with parameters.
8. Draw.

This section describes each of the aforementioned steps in some detail. The code snippets included here are part of a full, working sample that draws a single white square on the WebGL canvas. See the file *Chapter 1/example1-1.html* for a full code listing.

The Canvas and Drawing Context

All WebGL rendering takes place in a *context*, a JavaScript DOM object that provides the complete WebGL API. This structure mirrors the 2D drawing context provided in the HTML5 `<canvas>` tag. To get WebGL into your web page, create a `<canvas>` tag somewhere on the page, get the DOM object associated with it (say, using `document.getElementById()`), and then get a WebGL context for it. Example 1-1 shows how to get the WebGL context from a canvas DOM element.

Example 1-1. Obtaining a WebGL context from a canvas
```
function initWebGL(canvas) {
```

```
    var gl;
    try
    {
        gl = canvas.getContext("experimental-webgl");
    }
    catch (e)
    {
        var msg = "Error creating WebGL Context!: " + e.toString();
        alert(msg);
        throw Error(msg);
    }

    return gl;
}
```

 Note the try/catch block in the example. This is very important, because some browsers still do not support WebGL, or even if they do,
the user may not have the most recent version of that browser that
includes WebGL support. Further, even browsers that do support
WebGL may be running on old hardware, and not be able to give you
a valid WebGL rendering context. So, detection code like that in
Example 1-1 will help you with deploying a fallback such as a rendering
based on a 2D canvas—or at the very least, provide you with a graceful
exit.

The Viewport

Once you have obtained a valid WebGL drawing context from your canvas, you need
to tell it the rectangular bounds of where to draw. In WebGL, this is called a *viewport*.
Setting the viewport in WebGL is simple; just call the context's viewport() method (see
Example 1-2).

Example 1-2. Setting the WebGL viewport
```
function initViewport(gl, canvas)
{
    gl.viewport(0, 0, canvas.width, canvas.height);
}
```

Recall that the gl object used here was created by our helper function initWebGL(). In
this case, we have initialized the WebGL viewport to take up the entire contents of the
canvas's display area.

Buffers, ArrayBuffer, and Typed Arrays

Now we have a context ready for drawing. This is pretty much where the similarities to
the 2D Canvas end.

WebGL drawing is done with *primitives*—types of objects to draw such as triangle sets (arrays of triangles), triangle strips (described shortly), points, and lines. Primitives use arrays of data, called buffers, which define the positions of the vertices to be drawn. Example 1-3 shows how to create the vertex buffer data for a unit (1 × 1) square. The results are returned in a JavaScript object containing the vertex buffer data, the size of a vertex structure (in this case, three floating-point numbers to store *x*, *y*, and *z*), the number of vertices to be drawn, and the type of primitive that will be used to draw the square, in this example, a triangle strip. (A triangle strip is a rendering primitive that defines a sequence of triangles using the first three vertices for the first triangle, and each subsequent vertex in combination with the previous two for subsequent triangles.)

Example 1-3. Creating vertex buffer data

```
// Create the vertex data for a square to be drawn
function createSquare(gl) {
    var vertexBuffer;
    vertexBuffer = gl.createBuffer();
    gl.bindBuffer(gl.ARRAY_BUFFER, vertexBuffer);
    var verts = [
        .5,  .5,  0.0,
        -.5,  .5,  0.0,
        .5, -.5,  0.0,
        -.5, -.5,  0.0
    ];
    gl.bufferData(gl.ARRAY_BUFFER, new Float32Array(verts),
        gl.STATIC_DRAW);
    var square = {buffer:vertexBuffer, vertSize:3, nVerts:4,
        primtype:gl.TRIANGLE_STRIP};
    return square;
}
```

Note the use of the type `Float32Array`. This is a new data type introduced into web browsers for use with WebGL. `Float32Array` is a type of `ArrayBuffer`, also known as a *typed array*. This is a JavaScript type that stores compact binary data. Typed arrays can be accessed from JavaScript using the same syntax as ordinary arrays, but are much faster and consume less memory. They are ideal for use with binary data where performance is critical. Typed arrays can be put to general use, but their introduction into web browsers was pioneered by the WebGL effort. The latest typed array specification can be found on the Khronos website at *http://www.khronos.org/registry/typedarray/specs/latest/*.

Matrices

Before we can draw our square, we must create a couple of matrices. First, we need a matrix to define where the square is positioned in our 3D coordinate system, relative to the camera. This is known as a *ModelView matrix*, because it combines transformations of the model (3D mesh) and the camera. In our example, we are transforming the square by translating it along the negative z-axis (i.e., moving it away from the camera by −3.333 units).

The second matrix we need is the *projection matrix*, which will be required by our shader to convert the 3D space coordinates of the model in camera space into 2D coordinates drawn in the space of the viewport. In this example, the projection matrix defines a 45-degree field of view perspective camera. This matrix is pretty ugly; most people do not code projection matrices by hand, but use a library instead. There is a great open source library called *glMatrix* for doing matrix math in JavaScript (*https://github.com/toji/gl-matrix*). glMatrix is written by Brandon Jones, who is doing some wonderful WebGL work, including ports of *Quake* and other popular games.

Example 1-4 shows the code for setting up the ModelView and projection matrices.

Example 1-4. Setting up the ModelView and projection matrices

```
function initMatrices()
{
    // The transform matrix for the square - translate back in Z
    // for the camera
    modelViewMatrix = new Float32Array(
            [1, 0, 0, 0,
             0, 1, 0, 0,
             0, 0, 1, 0,
             0, 0, -3.333, 1]);

    // The projection matrix (for a 45 degree field of view)
        projectionMatrix = new Float32Array(
            [2.41421, 0, 0, 0,
             0, 2.41421, 0, 0,
             0, 0, -1.002002, -1,
             0, 0, -0.2002002, 0]);

}
```

The Shader

We are almost ready to draw our scene. There is one more important piece of setup: the shader. As described earlier, shaders are small programs, written in a high-level C-like language, that define how the pixels for 3D objects actually get drawn on the screen. WebGL requires the developer to supply a shader for each object that gets drawn. The shader can be used for multiple objects, so in practice it is often sufficient to supply one shader for the whole application, reusing it with different parameters each time.

A shader is typically composed of two parts: the *vertex shader* and the *fragment shader* (also known as the *pixel shader*). The vertex shader is responsible for transforming the coordinates of the object into 2D display space; the fragment shader is responsible for generating the final color output of each pixel for the transformed vertices, based on inputs such as color, texture, lighting, and material values. In our simple example, the vertex shader combines the `modelViewMatrix` and `projectionMatrix` values to create the final, transformed vertex for each input, and the fragment shader simply outputs a hardcoded white color.

In WebGL, shader setup requires a sequence of steps, including compiling the individual pieces, then linking them together. For brevity, we will show only the GLSL ES source for our two sample shaders (see Example 1-5), not the entire setup code. You can see exactly how the shaders are set up in the full sample.

Example 1-5. The vertex and fragment shaders
```
var vertexShaderSource =

    "    attribute vec3 vertexPos;\n" +
    "    uniform mat4 modelViewMatrix;\n" +
    "    uniform mat4 projectionMatrix;\n" +
    "    void main(void) {\n" +
    "        // Return the transformed and projected vertex value\n" +
    "        gl_Position = projectionMatrix * modelViewMatrix * \n" +
    "            vec4(vertexPos, 1.0);\n" +
    "    }\n";

var fragmentShaderSource =
    "    void main(void) {\n" +
    "        // Return the pixel color: always output white\n" +
    "        gl_FragColor = vec4(1.0, 1.0, 1.0, 1.0);\n" +
    "}\n";
```

Drawing Primitives

Now we are ready to draw our square (see Example 1-6). Our context has been created; our viewport has been set; our vertex buffer, matrices, and shader have been created and initialized. We define a function, `draw()`, which takes the WebGL context and our previously created square object. First, the function clears the canvas with a black background color. Then, it sets ("binds") the vertex buffer for the square to be drawn, sets ("uses") the shader to use, and connects up the vertex buffer and matrices to the shader as inputs. Finally, we call the WebGL `drawArrays()` method to draw the square. We simply tell it which type of primitives and how many vertices in the primitive; WebGL knows everything else already because we have essentially set those other items (vertices, matrices, shaders) as state in the context.

Example 1-6. The drawing code
```
function draw(gl, obj) {

    // clear the background (with black)
    gl.clearColor(0.0, 0.0, 0.0, 1.0);
    gl.clear(gl.COLOR_BUFFER_BIT);
```

```
    // set the vertex buffer to be drawn
    gl.bindBuffer(gl.ARRAY_BUFFER, obj.buffer);

    // set the shader to use
    gl.useProgram(shaderProgram);

    // connect up the shader parameters: vertex position and
    projection/model matrices
    gl.vertexAttribPointer(shaderVertexPositionAttribute,
        obj.vertSize, gl.FLOAT, false, 0, 0);
    gl.uniformMatrix4fv(shaderProjectionMatrixUniform, false,
        projectionMatrix);
    gl.uniformMatrix4fv(shaderModelViewMatrixUniform, false,
        modelViewMatrix);

    // draw the object
    gl.drawArrays(obj.primtype, 0, obj.nVerts);
}
```

The final output is shown in Figure 1-5.

Chapter Summary

Thus ends our nickel tour of a basic WebGL application. Whew! That was a lot of work. At this point, you might be thinking that was way too much work just to get a square on the screen. Heck, it's not even a 3D object! Well, I would be inclined to agree with you. WebGL programming, when done at this level, *is* work. The designers of the standard made a conscious decision to trade size for power. The API is small and simple, at the cost of having to do a lot of coding on the application side.

Obviously, in most cases, we won't be using WebGL just to draw 2D objects. The HTML5 2D Canvas would do just as well, with far fewer lines of code. But even when you are developing a true 3D application, it's a pretty tough slog if you code in this fashion. You will likely end up writing your own library on top of WebGL, or, better still, it would be really nice if other programmers had already done the hard work for you. Well, I have some good news: they have. In Chapter 2, we will build our first WebGL app using the Three.js library. Let's get to it.

Figure 1-5. A square drawn with WebGL

Your First WebGL Program

Now that we have covered the core concepts and, I hope, developed a basic understanding of the workings of WebGL, it is time to put that knowledge to use. In the next several chapters, we will create a series of WebGL sample pages, leading up to the development of a full application. Before we get going with that, we need to take a look at one more piece of our technology puzzle: Three.js.

Three.js—A JavaScript 3D Engine

Necessity is the mother of invention. It couldn't have been too long before somebody out there, dreading writing the same hundreds of lines of WebGL code over again, wrapped her work in a library that could be used for general-purpose 3D programming. In fact, several somebodies have done it. There are quite a few good open source libraries built for WebGL available, including GLGE (*http://www.glge.org/*), SceneJS (*http://www.scenejs.org/*), and CubicVR (*http://www.cubicvr.org/*). Each library does things a bit differently, but they share the goal of implementing high-level, developer-friendly features on top of raw WebGL.

The library we will use throughout this book is called *Three.js*, the creation of one Mr.doob, a.k.a. Ricardo Cabello Miguel, a programmer based in Barcelona, Spain. Three.js provides an easy, intuitive set of objects that are commonly found in 3D graphics. It is fast, using many best-practice graphics engine techniques. It is powerful, with several built-in object types and handy utilities. It is open source, hosted on GitHub, and well maintained, with several authors helping Mr.doob.

I chose Three.js to write the examples in this book for a couple of reasons. First, I am currently using it in my own development projects and really like it. Second, it is quite popular among these engines and is the perceived leader. You may find other libraries more to your liking, or better suited to the needs of your application. That's OK. One size definitely does *not* fit all here. The other engines I mentioned are great and have their place. You may even want to build your own engine if that's how you roll. But before you do, you should take a look at the great engine work already being done for WebGL.

The fact that toolkits like Three.js exist at all is due, in no small part, to how powerful web browsers' JavaScript virtual machines (VMs) have become in recent years. A few years back, VM performance would have made implementing such libraries prohibitive, and perhaps even made WebGL a nonstarter for practical use. Thankfully, today's VMs scream, and, with libraries like Three.js, WebGL has been made accessible to the millions of web developers on the planet.

Throughout the book, you will get to know Three.js in detail. For now, here is a summary of what it has to offer:

Three.js hides the details of 3D rendering
Three.js abstracts out the details of the WebGL API, representing the 3D scene as meshes, materials, and lights (i.e., the object types graphics programmers typically work with).

Three.js is object-oriented
Programmers work with first-class JavaScript objects instead of just making JavaScript function calls.

Three.js is feature-rich
More than just a wrapper around raw WebGL, Three.js contains many prebuilt objects useful for developing games, animations, presentations, high-resolution models, and special effects.

Three.js is fast
Three.js employs 3D graphics best practices to maintain high performance, without sacrificing usability.

Three.js supports interaction
WebGL provides no native support for picking (i.e., knowing when the mouse pointer is over an object). Three.js has solid picking support, making it easy to add interactivity to your applications.

Three.js does the math
Three.js has powerful, easy-to-use objects for 3D math, such as matrices, projections, and vectors.

Three.js has built-in file format support
You can load files in text formats exported by popular 3D modeling packages; there are also Three.js-specific JSON and binary formats.

Three.js is extensible
It is fairly easy to add features and customize Three.js. If you don't see a data type you need, write it and plug it in.

Three.js also works with the HTML5 2D canvas
As popular as WebGL has become, it is still not running everywhere. Three.js can also render most content into a 2D canvas, should the 3D canvas context not be available, allowing your code to gracefully fall back to another solution.

It is important to note a few things Three.js *doesn't* do. Three.js is not a game engine or virtual world platform. It lacks some of the commonly used features you would find in those systems, such as billboards, avatars, and physics. Nor does Three.js have the built-in network support you would expect if you were writing a multiplayer game. If you need those, you will have to build them yourself on top of Three.js. Still, its power and simplicity make Three.js a great choice for getting started on your WebGL journey.

So, without further ado, let's get going and write some code!

Setting Up Three.js

The first thing you will need to do is get the latest Three.js package from GitHub. As of this writing, the Three.js repository URL is *https://github.com/mrdoob/three.js/*. Once you have cloned the Git repository, you will want to use the minified version of the JavaScript located in *build/Three.js*. Hang on to the full source located under the *src* folder, too. The API documentation is linked from the GitHub page, but it is pretty basic, so you might want to have the source handy for reference.

 Three.js is built with the Google Closure Compiler; this one file contains the entire Three.js library built from several separate source files. If you are not familiar with Closure, and want to know more, go to *http://code.google.com/closure/compiler/*. If you don't want to deal with that, you can treat Three.js like a black box for now.

Take a little time with the source tree and documentation in order to familiarize yourself with Three.js. Now, if you're like me, you plan to ignore that recommendation because you are ready to jump right in. You're sick of the preliminaries and you want to get down to coding! OK, I understand—but at least do this for me: browse the examples. Under the folder *examples*, there are nearly 100 WebGL demos and several 2D canvas demos, too, covering a range of features and effects. You won't be sorry.

Finally, get all of this onto a web server. You will need to serve up your pages in order for most of the samples in the book to work. I run a local version of a standard LAMP stack on my MacBook…but all you really need is the "A" part of LAMP (i.e., a web server such as Apache).

A Simple Three.js Page

Now that you are set up, it's time to write your first WebGL program. From this exercise, you will see that it's pretty simple to get going with Three.js. Example 2-1 contains the complete code listing for a new version of that square-drawing program from Chapter 1, but in 30 lines instead of 150. Now the whole sample is greatly condensed.

Example 2-1. A simple page using Three.js

```
<!DOCTYPE html>
<html>
<head>
<title>A Simple Three.js Page</title>

    <script src="../libs/Three.js"></script>
    <script>
    function onLoad()
    {
        // Grab our container div
        var container = document.getElementById("container");

        // Create the Three.js renderer, add it to our div
        var renderer = new THREE.WebGLRenderer();
        renderer.setSize(container.offsetWidth, container.offsetHeight);
        container.appendChild( renderer.domElement );

        // Create a new Three.js scene
        var scene = new THREE.Scene();

        // Create a camera and add it to the scene
        var camera = new THREE.PerspectiveCamera( 45,
            container.offsetWidth / container.offsetHeight, 1, 4000 );
        camera.position.set( 0, 0, 3.3333 );
        scene.add( camera );

        // Now, create a rectangle and add it to the scene
        var geometry = new THREE.PlaneGeometry(1, 1);
        var mesh = new THREE.Mesh( geometry,
            new THREE.MeshBasicMaterial( ) );
        scene.add( mesh );

        // Render it
        renderer.render( scene, camera );
    }

    </script>

</head>

<body onLoad="onLoad();">
    <div id="container"
        style="width:500px; height:500px; background-color:#000000">
```

```
    </div>
  </body>

</html>
```

Let's walk through how it works.

First, we have a `<script>` tag that includes the Three.js library.

Then, we supply our script that draws the square. The entire program is contained in a single function, `onLoad()`, triggered by the page's `onLoad` event.

In the body of the function, we first find the page element that we are going to use to render the WebGL, and save that in the variable `container`. Then, we initialize the Three.js *renderer* object. The renderer is responsible for all Three.js drawing (via WebGL context, of course). We construct the renderer object, size it to the same size as the container, and add it as a DOM child element of the container.

Next, we create a *scene*. The scene is the top-level object in the Three.js graphics hierarchy. It contains all other graphical objects. (In Three.js, objects exist in a parent-child hierarchy. More on this in later chapters.) Once we have a scene, we are going to add a couple of objects to it: a camera and a mesh. The camera defines where we are viewing the scene from: in this example, we use a transform to set its `position` property to 3.3333 units (a little bit back) from the origin. Our mesh is composed of a geometry object and a material. For geometry, we are using a 1 × 1 rectangle created with the Three.js `PlaneGeometry` object. Our material tells Three.js how to shade the object. In this example, our material is of type `MeshBasicMaterial` (i.e., just a single simple color with a default value of pure white). Three.js objects have a default position of 0, 0, 0, so our white rectangle will be placed at the origin.

Finally, we need to render the scene. We do this by calling the renderer's `render()` method, feeding it a scene and a camera.

The output in Figure 2-1 should look familiar.

Note how Three.js closely mirrors the graphics concepts introduced in Chapter 1: we are working with objects (instead of buffers full of numbers), viewing them with a camera, moving them with transforms, and defining how they look with materials. In 30 lines of code, we have produced exactly the same graphic as our raw WebGL example that took 150 lines.

Figure 2-1. Square example, rewritten using Three.js

The savvy web programmer may notice a few unpalatable morsels in this example. First, the use of the onLoad event; in later chapters, we will move away from this model of detecting page loads and instead use jQuery's superior ready() method. Second, the entire program is contained in a single function; obviously we will not be building large programs this way. In later chapters, I will introduce a very simple framework for building modular programs with Three.js. Why all the kruft? For now, I am trying to keep the number of moving parts to a minimum, and the example as simple as possible. So, experienced engineers: please be patient for one more chapter; structured code is on the way.

A Real Example

At this point, you may be thinking, "Nice square," and starting to wonder if we are ever going to draw any *3D* graphics. Well, it's time. Example 2-2 shows how to replace our simple square with more interesting content—a page that looks nice and shows off major features of WebGL while still keeping it simple.

Figure 2-2 shows the page. We have some heading text, a cube with an image wrapped onto its faces, and some text at the bottom of the page. As the prompt suggests, the page is interactive: clicking within the canvas element toggles an animation that spins the cube.

Welcome to WebGL!

Click to animate the cube

Figure 2-2. A more involved Three.js example image from http://www.openclipart.org (CC0 Public Domain Dedication)

Let's take a detailed look at how all this is done. Example 2-2 contains the entire code listing. It's a little more involved than our first Three.js example, but still concise enough that we can walk through the whole example in short order.

Example 2-2. Welcome to WebGL!

```
<!DOCTYPE html>
<html>
<head>
<title>Welcome to WebGL</title>

    <link rel="stylesheet" href="../css/webglbook.css" />
    <script src="../libs/Three.js"></script>
    <script src="../libs/RequestAnimationFrame.js"></script>
    <script>

    var renderer = null,
        scene = null,
        camera = null,
        cube = null,
```

```
    animating = false;

function onLoad()
{
    // Grab our container div
    var container = document.getElementById("container");

    // Create the Three.js renderer, add it to our div
    renderer = new THREE.WebGLRenderer( { antialias: true } );
    renderer.setSize(container.offsetWidth, container.offsetHeight);
    container.appendChild( renderer.domElement );

    // Create a new Three.js scene
    scene = new THREE.Scene();

    // Put in a camera
    camera = new THREE.PerspectiveCamera( 45,
        container.offsetWidth / container.offsetHeight, 1, 4000 );
    camera.position.set( 0, 0, 3 );

    // Create a directional light to show off the object
    var light = new THREE.DirectionalLight( 0xffffff, 1.5);
    light.position.set(0, 0, 1);
    scene.add( light );

    // Create a shaded, texture-mapped cube and add it to the scene
    // First, create the texture map
    var mapUrl = "../images/molumen_small_funny_angry_monster.jpg";
    var map = THREE.ImageUtils.loadTexture(mapUrl);

    // Now, create a Phong material to show shading; pass in the map
    var material = new THREE.MeshPhongMaterial({ map: map });

    // Create the cube geometry
    var geometry = new THREE.CubeGeometry(1, 1, 1);

    // And put the geometry and material together into a mesh
    cube = new THREE.Mesh(geometry, material);

    // Turn it toward the scene, or we won't see the cube shape!
    cube.rotation.x = Math.PI / 5;
    cube.rotation.y = Math.PI / 5;

    // Add the cube to our scene
    scene.add( cube );

    // Add a mouse up handler to toggle the animation
    addMouseHandler();

    // Run our render loop
    run();
}
```

```
    function run()
    {
        // Render the scene
        renderer.render( scene, camera );

        // Spin the cube for next frame
        if (animating)
        {
            cube.rotation.y -= 0.01;
        }

        // Ask for another frame
        requestAnimationFrame(run);
    }

    function addMouseHandler()
    {
        var dom = renderer.domElement;

        dom.addEventListener( 'mouseup', onMouseUp, false);
    }

    function onMouseUp     (event)
    {
        event.preventDefault();

        animating = !animating;
    }

    </script>

</head>

<body onLoad="onLoad();" style="">
    <center><h1>Welcome to WebGL!</h1></center>
    <div id="container"
        style="width:95%; height:80%; position:absolute;">
    </div>
    <div id="prompt"
        style="width:95%; height:6%; bottom:0; position:absolute;">
    Click to animate the cube
    </div>
</body>

</html>
```

Other than a few setup details that I will talk about later on, and adding a stylesheet to control colors and fonts, this program starts out pretty much like the previous one. We create a Three.js renderer object and add its DOM element as a child of the container. This time, however, we pass a parameter in to the constructor, antialias, set to true, which tells Three.js to use *antialiased* rendering. Antialiasing avoids nasty artifacts that would make some drawn edges look jagged. (Note that Three.js has a couple of different styles for passing parameters to methods. Typically, constructor parameters are passed in an object with named fields, as in this example.) Then, we create a perspective camera, just as in the previous example. This time, the camera will be moved in a bit, so we get a nice close-up of the cube.

Shading the Scene

We are nearly ready to add our cube to the scene. If you peek ahead a few lines, you'll see that we create a unit cube using the Three.js `CubeGeometry` object. But before we add the cube, we need to do a few other things. First, we need to incorporate some *shading* into our scene. Without shading, you won't see the edges of the cube face. We will also need to create a texture map to render on the faces of the cube; we'll talk about that in just a bit.

To put shading into the scene, we will need to do two things: add a light source, and use a different kind of material for the cube. Lights come in a few different flavors in Three.js. In our example, we will use a *directional light*, a lighting source that illuminates in a specific direction but over an infinite distance (and doesn't have any particular location). The Three.js syntax is a little weird; instead of setting the direction, we are going to use the `position` attribute of the light to set it out from the origin; the direction is then inferred to point *into* the origin of the scene (i.e., at our cube).

The second thing we do is change the material we are using. The Three.js type `Mesh BasicMaterial` defines simple attributes such as a solid color and transparency. It will not display any shading based on our light sources. So we need to change this material to another type: `MeshPhongMaterial`. This material type implements a simple, fairly realistic-looking shading model (called "Phong shading") with high performance. (Three.js supports other, more sophisticated shading models that we will explore later.) With Phong shading in place, we are now able to see the edges of the cube. Cube faces that point more toward our light source are brightly lit; those that point away are less brightly lit. The edges are visible where any two faces meet.

 You may have noticed that, amid all the talk of shad*ing* in this section, I have made no mention of shad*ers*, those pesky little C-like programs I mentioned in Chapter 1 that WebGL requires in order to show bits on the screen. That's because Three.js implements them for us. We simply set up our lights and materials, and Three.js uses its built-in shaders to do the dirty work. Many thanks, Mr.doob!

Adding a Texture Map

Texture maps, also known as *textures*, are bitmaps used to represent surface attributes of 3D meshes. They can be used in simple ways to define just the color of a surface, or they can be combined to create complex effects such as bumps or highlights. WebGL provides several API calls for working with textures, and the standard provides for important security features, such as limiting cross-domain texture use (see Chapter 7 for more information). Happily, Three.js gives us a simple API for loading textures and associating them with materials without too much fuss. We call upon `THREE.ImageUtils.loadTexture()` to load the texture from an image file, and then associate the resultant texture with our material by setting the `map` parameter of the material's constructor.

Three.js is doing a lot of work under the covers here. It maps the bits of the JPEG image onto the correct parts of each cube face; the image isn't stretched around the cube, or upside down or backward on any of the faces. This might not seem like a big deal, but if you were to code something like this in raw WebGL, there would be a lot of details to get right. Three.js just knows. And once again, it is doing the hard work of the actual shading, with a built-in Phong shader program that combines the light values, material color, and pixels in the texture map to generate the correct color for each pixel and thus the finished image. There is a whole lot more we can do with textures in Three.js. We will be talking about it in more detail in subsequent chapters.

Now we are ready to create our cube mesh. We construct the geometry, the material, and the texture, and then put it all together into a Three.js mesh that we save into a variable named `cube`. The listing in Example 2-3 shows the lines of code involved in creating the lit, textured, and Phong-shaded cube.

Example 2-3. Creating the lit, textured, Phong-shaded cube

```
// Create a directional light to show off the object
var light = new THREE.DirectionalLight( 0xffffff, 1.5);
light.position.set(0, 0, 1);
scene.add( light );

// Create a shaded, texture-mapped cube and add it to the scene
// First, create the texture map
var mapUrl = "../images/molumen_small_funny_angry_monster.jpg";
var map = THREE.ImageUtils.loadTexture(mapUrl);

// Now, create a Phong material to show shading; pass in the map
var material = new THREE.MeshPhongMaterial({ map: map });

// Create the cube geometry
var geometry = new THREE.CubeGeometry(1, 1, 1);

// And put the geometry and material together into a mesh
cube = new THREE.Mesh(geometry, material);
```

Rotating the Object

Before we can see the cube in action, we need to do one more thing: rotate it a bit, or we would never know it was a cube—it would look exactly like our square from the previous example but with an image on it. So let's turn it on its x (horizontal)-axis toward the camera. We do that by setting the rotation property of the mesh. In Three.js, every object can have a position, a rotation, and a scale. (Remember how we used that in the first example to position the camera a little bit back from the square?) By assigning a nonzero value to rotation.x, we are telling Three.js to rotate by that amount around the object's x-axis. We do the same for the y-axis, turning the cube a little to the left. With these two rotations in place, we can see three of the six cube faces.

 Note the value we set for the rotations. Most 3D graphics systems represent degrees in units known as *radians*. Radians measure angles as the distance around the circumference of a unit square (i.e., 2π radians equals 360 degrees). Math.PI is equivalent to 180 degrees, thus the assignment mesh.rotation.x = Math.PI / 12 provides a 15-degree rotation about the x-axis.

The Run Loop and requestAnimationFrame()

You may have noticed a few structural changes between our first example and this one. First, we have added some helper functions. Second, we define a handful of global variables to tuck away information that will be used by the helper functions. (I know, I know: another hack. This will go away, as promised, when we move to a framework-centered approach in the next chapter.) We have also added a *run loop* (also known as a *render loop* or *simulation loop*). With a run loop, rather than rendering the scene only once, we render continually. This is not so important for a static scene, but if anything in the scene is animated or changes based on user input, we need to render continually. From here on, all our examples will render scenes using a run loop.

There are a couple of ways to implement a run loop. One way is to use setTimeout() with a callback that renders the scene and then resets the timeout. This is the classic web approach to animating; however, it is falling out of favor, because newer browsers support something better: requestAnimationFrame(). This function has been designed specifically for page animation, including animation with WebGL.

With requestAnimationFrame(), the browser can optimize performance because it will combine all such requests into a single redraw step. This function is not necessarily supported in all versions of all browsers, and—annoyingly—it has different names in different browsers. Therefore, I have incorporated a nice utility, *RequestAnimation Frame.js*, written by Paul Irish. This file supplies a cross-browser implementation of requestAnimationFrame().

We are ready to render our scene. We define a function, run( ), that implements the run loop. As before, we call the renderer's render( ) method, passing it the scene and the camera. Then, we have a little logic in there to support animating the cube. We will cover that part in the next section. Finally, we turn the crank by requesting another animation frame from the browser. See Example 2-4.

Example 2-4. The run loop
```
function run()
{
    // Render the scene
    renderer.render( scene, camera );

    // Spin the cube for next frame
    if (animating)
    {
        cube.rotation.y -= 0.01;
    }

    // Ask for another frame
    requestAnimationFrame(run);
}
```

The final result is shown in Figure 2-2. Now you can see the front and top of the cube. We have 3D on our web page!

Bringing the Page to Life

For a first full example, we could probably stop here. We have nice graphics on the page, and a true 3D object to look at. But at the end of the day, 3D graphics isn't just about the rendering; it's also about animation and interactivity. Otherwise, a web designer could just ask a 3D modeler friend to render a still image out of 3ds Max or Maya, stick it in the page with an <img> tag, and be done with it. But that's not the whole story. With that in mind, we put animation and interactivity in even our simplest example. Here's how.

In the preceding section, we discussed the run loop. This is our opportunity to make changes to the scene before we render the next frame. To spin a cube, we need to change its rotation value with each frame. We don't want the thing tumbling around randomly; rather, we would like a smooth rotation around its (vertical) y-axis, and so we just add a little to the rotation's y value each time around. This style represents one of the simpler ways to animate WebGL content. There are several other approaches, each of varying complexity. We will get to those in a later chapter.

Finally, it would be nice to control when the cube spins. We have added a click handler to the page, using straightforward DOM event methods. The only trick is to figure out where to add the click event handler. In this case, we use the DOM element associated with the Three.js renderer object. See the code listing in Example 2-5.

Example 2-5. Adding mouse interaction
```
function addMouseHandler()
{
    var dom = renderer.domElement;

    dom.addEventListener( 'mouseup', onMouseUp, false);
}

function onMouseUp    (event)
{
    event.preventDefault();

    animating = !animating;
}
```
Click on the cube. Watch it spin. Hypnotic, isn't it?

Chapter Summary

Well, there is our first real example. I have to say that it was pretty painless. In a few pages of code, we were able to create a standard HTML page with 3D content, pretty it up, give it life with animation, and make it interactive. In the past, there was no way to do that. But the pieces have all come together with WebGL. And with Three.js, you don't need a graduate degree in computer graphics to do it.

We're up and running. The rest is just details.

CHAPTER 3

Graphics

At the heart of WebGL lies a high-performance system for rendering graphics using a computer's 3D graphics processing unit, or GPU. As we saw in the first two chapters, the WebGL API gets pretty close to that metal to give developers full control and power, while libraries like Three.js provide a more intuitive layer for managing what gets rendered. In the next several chapters, we are going to use Three.js to explore essential WebGL development concepts. Let's begin that exploration by taking a close look at graphics.

Graphics comprises several related topics: meshes and other drawn primitives, such as points and lines; matrices and the transformation hierarchy; texture maps; and shading, including materials and lights. It's a big area to cover, and to do it justice we are going to create a series of examples as big as the topic itself: we're going to build a model of the solar system. See Figure 3-1 for a sneak peek.

There is a lot going on here: richly textured planets in orbit around a blazing sun; satellites and rings around planets; a star field background; and lines tracing the planetary orbits. In putting this model together, we will get a points-of-interest grand tour of developing graphics with WebGL.

 In case it's not obvious, the solar system depicted combines a certain amount of photorealism—the planet texture maps come from real satellite and telescope pictures—plus annotative drawing, changes in scale, and other cheats (such as spheres for planets instead of ellipsoids) in order to depict the entire system on a page. The goal here is to illustrate, not to simulate reality with any precision. If you are interested in a more realistic space simulator, there are already some great ones on the market.

Figure 3-1. Solar system model; planet texture maps courtesy NASA/JPL-Caltech and Bjorn Jonsson

Sim.js—A Simple Simulation Framework for WebGL

Before we create our stellar sample, we are going to talk briefly about one other topic. Three.js provides a nice layer to insulate the gritty details of the WebGL API. However, in everyday use, you will quickly find yourself performing the same Three.js tasks over and over, and contemplate creating a framework to simplify your life. Have a look at the samples you downloaded with Three.js and you'll see what I mean: line after line of code to create meshes, add them as children of other objects, set textures, add DOM event callbacks to handle clicking, and so on. Many of these tasks could be wrapped into a higher-level set of reusable objects. Understandably, this is outside the scope of the Three.js mission, so no criticism is intended of Mr.doob's toolkit; the job falls on us as application writers.

The examples for this chapter and all chapters that follow are built using *Sim.js*, a simulation framework of my creation. Sim.js is a tiny library—just a few pages of code and a handful of classes—that wraps the more repetitive Three.js tasks such as renderer setup, the run loop, DOM event handling, basic parent-child hierarchy operations, and input. A copy of the source to Sim.js is included with this book, and can also be found on GitHub at *https://github.com/tparisi/Sim.js*. The code in Sim.js is almost self-explanatory, but let's take a minute to look at its key features to set the stage for our examples:

The Publisher class (`Sim.Publisher`)

This class is the base for any object that generates ("publishes") events. Whenever an interesting event happens, `Sim.Publisher` iterates through its list of registered callbacks, calling each with the event data and the supplied object ("*subscriber*"). `Sim.Publisher` is the base class for most Sim.js objects.

The Application class (`Sim.App`)

This class wraps all the Three.js setup/teardown code for a page, such as the creation of the renderer, the top-level scene object, and the camera. It also adds DOM handlers to the Three.js rendering canvas to handle resizing, mouse input, and other events. `Sim.App` also manages the list of individual objects for the application, and implements the run loop.

The Object class (`Sim.Object`)

This is the base class for most of the objects in an application. It manages the state for a single (application-defined) object, and handles a few Three.js basics, including adding/removing the object from the scene, adding/removing children from the object hierarchy (more on this shortly), and setting/retrieving standard Three.js properties such as position, scale, and rotation.

 I built Sim.js primarily to illustrate WebGL concepts for this book. It is a bit too simplistic for building large-scale applications or games, but you may still find it useful in your development work. Feel free to improve upon it and send me feedback.

That's pretty much all there is to Sim.js. With this simple set of helper code in place, we are now ready to proceed to building the samples.

Creating Meshes

The most commonly used type of rendered object in WebGL is the *mesh*. A mesh is composed of a set of polygons (typically triangles or quadrangles), each described by three or more 3D vertices. Meshes can be as simple as a single triangle, or extremely complex, with enough detail to fully depict a real-world object such as a car, airplane, or person. We will use several meshes in our solar system model, primarily spheres for the planet shapes. Three.js has a built-in sphere object, so there is no need to create spheres by hand.

We are going to build our full solar system in several steps. Let's start by creating a familiar object: the Earth. Example 3-1 shows the code listing for a first Earth application. In this example, we create a sphere with a single high-resolution texture map based on satellite photographs of the planet. Launch the file *Chapter 3/graphics-earth-basic.html*. The result is shown in Figure 3-2.

Example 3-1. Basic Earth example

```
 // Constructor
EarthApp = function()
{
    Sim.App.call(this);
}

// Subclass Sim.App
EarthApp.prototype = new Sim.App();

// Our custom initializer
EarthApp.prototype.init = function(param)
{
    // Call superclass init code to set up scene, renderer,
    default camera
    Sim.App.prototype.init.call(this, param);

    // Create the Earth and add it to our sim
    var earth = new Earth();
    earth.init();
    this.addObject(earth);
}

// Custom Earth class
Earth = function()
{
    Sim.Object.call(this);
}

Earth.prototype = new Sim.Object();

Earth.prototype.init = function()
{
    // Create our Earth with nice texture
    var earthmap = "./images/earth_surface_2048.jpg";
    var geometry = new THREE.SphereGeometry(1, 32, 32);
    var texture = THREE.ImageUtils.loadTexture(earthmap);
    var material = new THREE.MeshBasicMaterial( { map: texture } );
    var mesh = new THREE.Mesh( geometry, material );

    // Let's work in the tilt
    mesh.rotation.z = Earth.TILT;

    // Tell the framework about our object
    this.setObject3D(mesh);
}

Earth.prototype.update = function()
{
    // "I feel the Earth move..."
    this.object3D.rotation.y += Earth.ROTATION_Y;
```

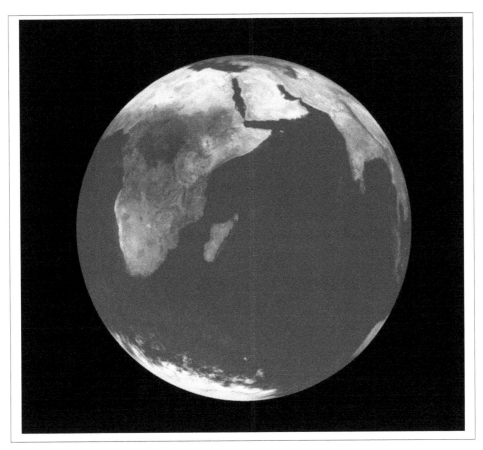

Figure 3-2. Your world, rendered

```
}
```

```
Earth.ROTATION_Y = 0.0025;
Earth.TILT = 0.41;
```

The source for this example is in file *Chapter 3/earth-basic.js*. This file defines two objects: a custom subclass of `Sim.App` called `EarthApp`, and an `Earth` object derived from `Sim.Object`. These are all we need for our simple example. Let's take a walk through it.

The HTML file for this example (not shown in the listing) creates a new instance of `EarthApp`, calls its `init()` method to do all the setup, and then calls `run()` (i.e. the run loop). From there, the rest happens automatically, driven by each animation frame.

The `EarthApp` object is quite simple. Its `init()` method creates an instance of an `Earth`, adds it to its list of objects, and returns. Everything else in `EarthApp` is inherited from `Sim.App`. Under the covers, in each frame of the run loop, we call `update()`, and then tell Three.js to render the scene. `update()` iterates through the application's list of objects, calling `update()` on each of them in turn.

Our `Earth` class defines a couple of custom methods. First, `init()` is responsible for creating the Earth mesh. In Three.js, a mesh is composed of a geometry object and a material. For the geometry, we create a highly detailed Three.js sphere (type `THREE.SphereGeometry`) of radius 1. The second and third parameters tell Three.js how many triangles to generate by providing a number of cross sections and triangles per cross section. In this example, we are looking at Earth up close, so we want a high-resolution version. (Play around with these parameters, and you will see that if you make the values low enough, your spheres will look more like golf balls. For some applications, this can be fine, especially if the object is far away from the camera.) To get a sense of the vertex data that underlies a sphere, Figure 3-3 shows our geometry rendered as a *wireframe* (i.e. with the polygon outlines drawn instead of the surface). You can clearly see the quadrangles ("quads") that comprise our sphere geometry.

In order to actually see our sphere mesh, we also have to define a *material*, an object that describes the surface properties of the rendered mesh. In Three.js, materials can have several parameters, including a base color, transparency, and reflectivity. Materials may also include one or more *texture maps* (also known simply as *textures*), bitmaps used to represent various surface attributes. Textures can be used in simple ways to define just the color of a surface, or they can be combined to create complex effects such as bumps or highlights. In this first example, we will keep it simple and use a high-resolution satellite image of the Earth for our texture. We create a texture object from the image file using the Three.js utility function `THREE.ImageUtils.loadTexture()`. The texture map for our Earth's surface is shown in Figure 3-4.

Note that this image is a projection of 3D surface data into a 2D bitmap. It has been designed for use as a texture wrapped onto a sphere. Three.js contains the logic for mapping locations within the 2D texture (known as *UV coordinates*; see later in this chapter) to vertex positions on the sphere mesh, so we don't have to.

You may have noticed that our sample Earth looks a bit flat. That is because of the type of material we are using. In this example, we use `THREE.MeshBasicMaterial`, a type that does not employ any shading at all. This material type simply paints the pixels supplied in the texture map, or if there is none, it uses the color value of the material.

We know we can do better than this in rendering our planet—and we will in the next section. I showed you this method here by way of illustrating WebGL's great flexibility in rendering styles. You can render with fully realistic lighting, or if you choose, you can render your models as in Example 3-1, a rendering style known as *unlit*, or alternatively, *prelit*. (Confusing terminology, I know. But the idea behind *prelit* rendering is that the

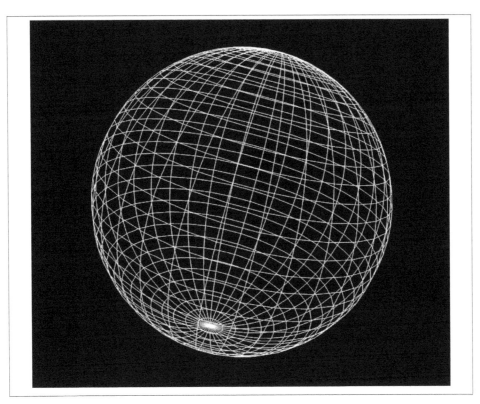

Figure 3-3. Wireframe rendering of a sphere

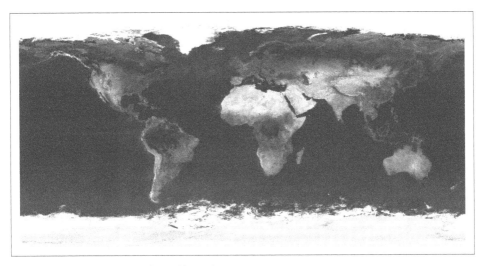

Figure 3-4. Texture map of Earth's surface

lighting has been precomputed into the texture prior to runtime and thus does not have to be computed by the renderer; it simply renders the precomputed values with no additional lighting effects needing to be calculated at runtime.) In our example, pre-lighting the model doesn't look so great, but for some applications, it is just what you want.

To complete the setup, our init() method sets a rotation value on the mesh (for the tilt of the Earth's axis), and calls the inherited setObject3D() method so that the framework knows what Three.js object it is dealing with. Finally, our Earth object's custom update() method rotates the sphere by a predefined amount each time, simulating the Earth's rotation so that we can get a good look at the whole planet.

Using Materials, Textures, and Lights

The preceding example illustrated the simplest way that we can render a textured model in Three.js, using a basic material, a single texture, and no lighting. In this section, we are going to explore using materials, textures, and lights in various ways to add more realism to our Earth. First, we are going to light the model, to simulate how the sun's rays reach the Earth across space. Figure 3-5 shows a lit version of the Earth in which we can see gradations of shading across the surface of the sphere. To run this example, load *Chapter 3/graphics-earth-lit.html* in your browser.

On the left side, we see the Arabian Peninsula and Africa brightly lit; toward the front, the Indian Ocean shows shiny highlights; on the right, East Asia and Australia recede into darkness. We create this effect by placing a light source a bit out of the scene and to the left. Let's talk about the light and material types Three.js provides for doing this.

Types of Lights

Three.js supports several different types of lights. There are *ambient lights*, which provide constant illumination throughout the scene, regardless of position; *point lights*, which emanate from a particular position in all directions, and illuminate over a certain distance; *spot lights*, which emanate from a particular position and in a specific direction, over a certain distance (and look a lot like spotlights you see in the movies); and finally, *directional lights*, which illuminate in a specific direction but over an infinite distance (and don't have any particular position).

Our real sun emits light in all directions, so for our simulated sun, we will choose a point light. Because we have a nice framework for making new Three.js objects and adding them to the scene, let's take advantage of it by creating another Sim.Object subclass called Sun. The listing in Example 3-2 contains excerpts from the file *earth-lit.js* that implement this new class and add it to the EarthApp simulation.

Figure 3-5. Earth with lighting

Example 3-2. Lighting the Earth

```
// Our custom initializer
EarthApp.prototype.init = function(param)
{
    // Call superclass init code to set up scene, renderer,
    default camera
    Sim.App.prototype.init.call(this, param);

    // Create the Earth and add it to our sim
    var earth = new Earth();
    earth.init();
    this.addObject(earth);

    // Let there be light!
    var sun = new Sun();
    sun.init();
    this.addObject(sun);
}

...

Earth.prototype.init = function()
{
```

```
    // Create our Earth with nice texture
    var earthmap = "./images/earth_surface_2048.jpg";
    var geometry = new THREE.SphereGeometry(1, 32, 32);
    var texture = THREE.ImageUtils.loadTexture(earthmap);
    var material = new THREE.MeshPhongMaterial( { map: texture } );
    var mesh = new THREE.Mesh( geometry, material );

    // Let's work in the tilt
    mesh.rotation.z = Earth.TILT;

    // Tell the framework about our object
    this.setObject3D(mesh);
}

...

// Custom Sun class
Sun = function()
{
    Sim.Object.call(this);
}

Sun.prototype = new Sim.Object();

Sun.prototype.init = function()
{
    // Create a point light to show off the earth - set the light
    out back and to left a bit
    var light = new THREE.PointLight( 0xffffff, 2, 100);
    light.position.set(-10, 0, 20);

    // Tell the framework about our object
    this.setObject3D(light);
}
```

In EarthApp.init(), we add the lines of code to create our sun, shown in boldface. In the Earth initialization, we substitute a new kind of material: namely, THREE.Mesh PhongMaterial. This material type implements a simple, fairly realistic-looking shading model (called "Phong shading") with high performance. With this in place, we can now light our model. (In fact, we *have to* light our model: the Three.js built-in Phong material requires a light source, or we won't see anything.)

The remainder of the listing shows the implementation of the Sun class. We create a point light, and locate it to the left (negative x) and out of the screen a bit (positive z). Then, we add it to the scene, just like we did with our Earth mesh. (In Three.js, lights are first-class objects, just like meshes. That makes it easy to move and otherwise transform their properties.) Now our Earth is lit and is starting to look more like the real thing.

At this point, it might be worth reminding you that lights and materials are *not* built-in features of WebGL; rather, all the so-called material properties rendered in a WebGL scene are the result of executing one or more shaders. Materials and lights are, however, common concepts in 3D graphics, and much of the value provided in a toolkit like Three.js lies in its built-in shaders that implement material in a way that most developers can use them out of the box.

Creating Serious Realism with Multiple Textures

Our Earth model is looking pretty good, but we can do even better. The real Earth has elevation—mountains and such that can be seen from a distance. It also has a wide range of bright and dark areas. And of course, the Earth has an atmosphere with clouds that are continually in motion. With just a bit more work, we can add these features and experience a much more realistic Earth, as depicted in Figure 3-6 (file *Chapter 3/ graphics-earth-shader.html*).

Figure 3-6. Earth rendered using multiple textures

Note the apparent elevations on the Eurasian land mass and Indonesia. Also, in the live example—not so much in the screenshot—you can see that some spots are much shinier than in the preceding version, especially inland bodies of water. Finally, we see a cloud layer that, when you are running the live example, moves slowly against the backdrop of the Earth's surface. Now that is one beautiful planet!

Knowing what you know now about meshes and polygons, you might be tempted to think that this detailed goodness comes from heaping on more polygons—perhaps thousands of them. But it doesn't. We can achieve this high level of realism by simply using a new material type and a few more textures. In addition to the built-in materials we have seen thus far, Three.js provides a general-purpose type called THREE.Shader Material. As the name implies, this material allows the developer to supply a shader program along with other parameters. But don't freak out—we don't have to write a shader program ourselves; Three.js provides a small library of prebuilt ones that implement some of the more common effects. To create our highly realistic view of the Earth, including elevations and shiny highlights, we are going to employ three texture maps:

A color map (also known as a diffuse map)
> This provides the base pixel color (i.e., the satellite imagery of the Earth's surface we used in the previous version; see Figure 3-3).

A normal map (otherwise known as a bump map)
> Normal maps are essentially encodings of additional mesh attributes, known as *normals*, into bitmap data as RBG values. Normals determine how much light bounces off a mesh's surface, resulting in lighter or darker areas depending on the value. Normals create the "bumpiness" of the Earth in a much more compact and high-performance format than defining another vertex for each elevation. The normal map for our Earth is shown in Figure 3-7. Compare this map to the quads depicted in our wireframe drawing of the Earth sphere in Figure 3-3; it is of a much higher resolution. By encoding elevations in normal maps, we can save vertex memory in our meshes, and improve rendering performance.

A specular map
> The term *specular highlights,* or *specular reflection,* refers to how much and what color light bounces off a mesh's surface. Similar to normal maps, the specular map is a more efficient encoding of these values. The specular map we use to define shiny areas of the Earth is shown in Figure 3-8. Lighter RBG values represent shinier areas; darker values, less shiny.

Figure 3-7. Earth elevations using a normal map

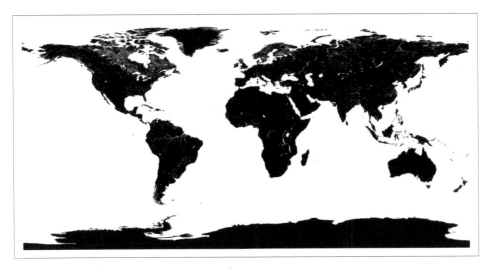

Figure 3-8. Earth shininess using a specular map

Let's take a look at the changes we made to our `Earth` class to get these effects. The code listing in Example 3-3 shows the relevant bits from source file *Chapter 3/earth-shader.js*.

Example 3-3. Earth rendered with multiple textures

```
Earth.prototype.init = function()
{
    // Create a group to contain Earth and Clouds
    var earthGroup = new THREE.Object3D();
```

```javascript
    // Tell the framework about our object
    this.setObject3D(earthGroup);

    // Add the earth globe and clouds
    this.createGlobe();
    this.createClouds();
}

Earth.prototype.createGlobe = function()
{
    // Create our Earth with nice texture - normal map for elevation,
    specular highlights
    var surfaceMap = THREE.ImageUtils.loadTexture(
        "./images/earth_surface_2048.jpg" );
    var normalMap = THREE.ImageUtils.loadTexture(
        "./images/earth_normal_2048.jpg" );
    var specularMap = THREE.ImageUtils.loadTexture(
        "./images/earth_specular_2048.jpg" );

    var shader = THREE.ShaderUtils.lib[ "normal" ],
    uniforms = THREE.UniformsUtils.clone( shader.uniforms );

    uniforms[ "tNormal" ].texture = normalMap;
    uniforms[ "tDiffuse" ].texture = surfaceMap;
    uniforms[ "tSpecular" ].texture = specularMap;

    uniforms[ "enableDiffuse" ].value = true;
    uniforms[ "enableSpecular" ].value = true;

    var shaderMaterial = new THREE.ShaderMaterial({
        fragmentShader: shader.fragmentShader,
        vertexShader: shader.vertexShader,
        uniforms: uniforms,
        lights: true
    });

    var globeGeometry = new THREE.SphereGeometry(1, 32, 32);

    // We'll need these tangents for our shader
    globeGeometry.computeTangents();
    var globeMesh = new THREE.Mesh( globeGeometry, shaderMaterial );

    // Let's work in the tilt
    globeMesh.rotation.z = Earth.TILT;

    // Add it to our group
    this.object3D.add(globeMesh);

    // Save it away so we can rotate it
    this.globeMesh = globeMesh;
}
```

```
Earth.prototype.createClouds = function()
{
    // Create our clouds
    var cloudsMap = THREE.ImageUtils.loadTexture(
        "./images/earth_clouds_1024.png" );
    var cloudsMaterial = new THREE.MeshLambertMaterial(
        { color: 0xffffff, map: cloudsMap, transparent:true } );

    var cloudsGeometry = new THREE.SphereGeometry(Earth.CLOUDS_SCALE,
        32, 32);
    cloudsMesh = new THREE.Mesh( cloudsGeometry, cloudsMaterial );
    cloudsMesh.rotation.z = Earth.TILT;

    // Add it to our group
    this.object3D.add(cloudsMesh);

    // Save it away so we can rotate it
    this.cloudsMesh = cloudsMesh;
}

Earth.prototype.update = function()
{
    // "I feel the Earth move..."
    this.globeMesh.rotation.y += Earth.ROTATION_Y;

    // "Clouds, too..."
    this.cloudsMesh.rotation.y += Earth.CLOUDS_ROTATION_Y;

    Sim.Object.prototype.update.call(this);
}

Earth.ROTATION_Y = 0.001;
Earth.TILT = 0.41;
Earth.CLOUDS_SCALE = 1.005;
Earth.CLOUDS_ROTATION_Y = Earth.ROTATION_Y * 0.95;
```

First, we have broken out the initialization into a few helper functions because it's getting a bit more involved. We have also changed our base Three.js object from a single mesh to a different type: THREE.Object3D. This class is a base type inherited by other Three.js objects we have already seen, such as meshes, lights, and cameras. THREE.Object3D contains position, orientation, and scale properties used by all of these types; in addition, it can contain a list of *children*: other Three.js objects that will move, rotate, and scale along with it when those properties are changed. We are going to talk about this in more detail when we discuss the transform hierarchy a little later. For now, we are using Object3D just to contain a couple of other objects, namely the Earth sphere and a second sphere used to depict the cloud layer.

Now on to the exciting part: the shader that implements normal mapping and specular highlights. For this, we call on THREE.ShaderUtils. This utility class contains a library of prebuilt shader programs. In this case, we will use the normal mapping shader contained in `THREE.ShaderUtils.lib["normal"]`. We then create an object called `uniforms` that contains several named properties; these are the parameters to the shader program. (The terminology *uniforms* has a very specific meaning with shaders; we will cover this and other shader topics a little later on.) The normal mapping shader requires at least a normal map texture to compute the bumps; we supply that texture, plus the diffuse and specular texture maps. We also set a couple of flags to tell the shader to also use the diffuse and specular values in the computed result. (These flags are off by default; try setting them to `false` and see what happens.)

With our shader program in place, we can create the `THREE.ShaderMaterial` for our mesh, using our normal mapping shader program, the uniform parameters, and telling the shader to use lighting. We must do one more thing for the shader to work properly: compute *tangents*. Tangents are additional vectors required for each vertex in order to compute normal mapping values. Three.js does not calculate tangents for geometries by default, so we have to take this explicit step in this case. Once our geometry is set up, we create a mesh and add it as a child of our group. And that's it—we have a normal-mapped Earth with specular highlights. Sweet!

Textures and Transparency

Continuing with Example 3-3, we want to add our cloud layer. This involves employing another weapon in our arsenal: using textures with transparency. Just as with 2D web graphics, WebGL supports textures with an alpha channel in PNG format. But in WebGL, that texture can be mapped onto any kind of object, and drawn so that the transparent bits expose other objects behind it (i.e., WebGL supports *alpha blending*). Three.js makes this pretty easy to deal with by simply supplying a PNG with alpha and setting the `transparent` flag of the material being used. Let's have a look.

The helper method `createClouds()` builds a second sphere, this one just a bit bigger than the Earth. Then, we create a material with transparency turned on. Note that we are using a material type we haven't seen before: `MeshLambertMaterial`. In Lambert shading, the apparent brightness of the surface to an observer is the same regardless of the observer's angle of view. This works really well for clouds, which broadly diffuse the light that strikes them. We put these together, and add them as a second child of our group. Finally, during `update()`, we spin our cloud mesh at a slightly slower rate than the globe and—*voilà!*—a cloud layer moving gently across the Earth.

Building a Transform Hierarchy

Now that we know how to create meshes and make them look nice, let's take a look at how to move them around using *transforms*. Transforms allow us to position, orient, and scale objects without having to operate directly on their vertices. Recall our Earth examples thus far. To spin the globe, we didn't loop through the sphere geometry's vertex positions, moving each one; rather, we changed a single `rotation` property on the mesh, and the entire Earth rotated.

Take this concept a step further: many graphics systems, including Three.js, support the concept of a *transform hierarchy*, wherein transforming an object transforms all its children, too. We can think of the transform hierarchy as analogous to the DOM parent-child hierarchy, though the comparison is imprecise. As with DOM elements, adding an object to a scene adds all its children; likewise, removing an object removes its children. However, a classic transform hierarchy in 3D graphics does not have the various layout capabilities of a DOM hierarchy, such as document-relative and absolute positioning. Instead, 3D transform hierarchies typically use parent-relative positioning, and we will exploit this capability to our advantage.

In Three.js, every instance of `Object3D` has position, rotation, and scale properties. Under the covers, these values are converted into an internally stored *matrix* that is used to calculate the screen-space positions of the vertices at rendering time. For any child of an `Object3D`, its matrix values are multiplied together with its parent's, and so on, all the way up the parent-child hierarchy to the root. So, whenever you move, rotate, or scale an object in Three.js, it moves, rotates, or scales all its children, too.

We are going to create one last, small example before we dive into building the full solar system. Let's add a moon orbiting our Earth, using a transform hierarchy. You will see that setting it up this way makes simple work of an otherwise hard problem. In addition, this structure prepares us so that we can drop our Earth model into a full planetary system, and, thanks to the magic of the transform hierarchy, it will just work. Example 3-4 shows an excerpt from the Earth/moon system implemented in *Chapter 3/earth-moon.js*. You can run the example by loading the file *Chapter 3/graphics-earth-moon.html*.

Example 3-4. Earth and moon transform hierarchy
```
Earth.prototype.init = function()
{
    // Create a group to contain Earth and Clouds
    var earthGroup = new THREE.Object3D();

    // Tell the framework about our object
    this.setObject3D(earthGroup);

    // Add the earth globe and clouds
    this.createGlobe();
    this.createClouds();

    // Add the moon
    this.createMoon();
}
```

```
...

Earth.prototype.createMoon = function()
{
    var moon = new Moon();
    moon.init();
    this.addChild(moon);
}
...
// Custom Moon class
Moon = function()
{
    Sim.Object.call(this);
}

Moon.prototype = new Sim.Object();

Moon.prototype.init = function()
{
    var MOONMAP = "./images/moon_1024.jpg";

    var geometry = new THREE.SphereGeometry(Moon.SIZE_IN_EARTHS,
        32, 32);
    var texture = THREE.ImageUtils.loadTexture(MOONMAP);
    var material = new THREE.MeshPhongMaterial( { map: texture,
        ambient:0x888888 } );
    var mesh = new THREE.Mesh( geometry, material );

    // Let's get this into earth-sized units (earth is a unit sphere)
    var distance = Moon.DISTANCE_FROM_EARTH / Earth.RADIUS;
    mesh.position.set(Math.sqrt(distance / 2), 0,
        -Math.sqrt(distance / 2));

    // Rotate the moon so it shows its moon-face toward earth
    mesh.rotation.y = Math.PI;

    // Create a group to contain Earth and Satellites
    var moonGroup = new THREE.Object3D();
    moonGroup.add(mesh);

    // Tilt to the ecliptic
    moonGroup.rotation.x = Moon.INCLINATION;

    // Tell the framework about our object
    this.setObject3D(moonGroup);

    // Save away our moon mesh so we can rotate it
    this.moonMesh = mesh;
}

Moon.prototype.update = function()
{
```

```
    // Moon orbit
    this.object3D.rotation.y += (Earth.ROTATION_Y / Moon.PERIOD);

    Sim.Object.prototype.update.call(this);
}

Moon.DISTANCE_FROM_EARTH = 356400;
Moon.PERIOD = 28;
Moon.EXAGGERATE_FACTOR = 1.2;
Moon.INCLINATION = 0.089;
Moon.SIZE_IN_EARTHS = 1 / 3.7 * Moon.EXAGGERATE_FACTOR;
```

First, we create a new object class, Moon, to represent our moon. The Earth's initialization method calls a helper, createMoon(), to create an instance of the moon and add it as a child of itself. Under the covers, Sim.Object.addChild() adds the object's private Three.js Object3D as a child of its own Object3D—that is, the Three.js magic for wiring up the transform hierarchy. In addition, our moon has itself created another internal Three.js object, moonGroup, into which it adds the moon mesh. This might seem like overkill—the group is only going to contain one mesh, so why create an extra group? But in fact, we are going to make use of this extra object in a moment.

To place the moon where it belongs, we position the mesh. Note that in our previous examples, we have never set the Earth's position explicitly. By default, objects are placed at the origin (0, 0, 0), so in this case, the Earth is centered at the origin. We position the moon mesh at its proper distance from the Earth, in Earth-sized units. We also set up a few rotations so that the moon sits at its proper angle to the Earth, with its well-known face showing toward us.

Now, we are ready to discuss how the transform hierarchy comes into play. First, by making the moon a child of the Earth, we can reuse this code in other simulations such as a full solar system: whenever the Earth wanders its way around the solar system, because it is a child, the moon will follow. Second, because we have created an internal transform hierarchy for the moon itself, we can easily accomplish a fairly complex operation, namely having the moon orbit around the Earth. Here's how it works: the moonGroup object contains a mesh; the mesh is positioned at a certain distance from the Earth using the mesh's transform properties. By rotating the group, not the mesh, we can move the moon in a circular orbit around the Earth, with its familiar face always facing toward Earth, just as it does in real life. (Well, almost; we all know that the true orbit of the moon is quite elliptical. But that's a bigger kettle of fish. For our purposes here, we are happy to cheat with a circle.) If we had simply created the mesh and not the containing group, then when we rotated the mesh it would literally rotate (i.e., spin in place) and not orbit the Earth. Figure 3-9 shows our nearest celestial neighbor, caught in the act.

Figure 3-9. The moon in orbit around the Earth

Creating Custom Geometry

Let's continue our journey outward past the moon. For the remainder of this chapter, we will be using the full solar system example, which can be found in *Chapter 3/graphics-solar-system.html* and its associated files.

Our simple solar system model incorporates the Earth-moon system but no other planetary satellites. We can live without those, and other distinguishing bodies in the solar system such as the asteroid belt—but it would be hard to build a believable orrery without troubling with one additional bauble: Saturn's rings.

While Three.js has a rich set of prebuilt geometry types, it does not include something that can pass for Saturn's rings. Essentially we need a disc with a hole in it, that we can texture with some transparency to emulate the look of the rings. Three.js has a built-in torus object, but no matter how you try to flatten using scaling or other tricks, it looks like a donut, not a disc. So, it appears that we will need to make our own geometry. We could go about this in one of two ways: either (1) create a model using a modeling package such as Blender or 3ds Max and export it to one of several formats Three.js knows how to load; or (2) create the geometry in code by building a custom subclass of THREE.Geometry. Because we are going to cover 3D modeling packages in a later chapter, let's have a look at how to customize Three.js by building our own geometry class. Example 3-5 shows the code, which can be found in the file *Chapter 3/saturn.js*.

Example 3-5. Custom Geometry class for Saturn's rings

```
// The rings
Saturn.Rings = function ( innerRadius, outerRadius, nSegments ) {

    THREE.Geometry.call( this );

    var outerRadius = outerRadius || 1,
    innerRadius = innerRadius || .5,
    gridY = nSegments || 10;

    var i, twopi = 2 * Math.PI;
    var iVer = Math.max( 2, gridY );

    var origin = new THREE.Vector3(0, 0, 0);
    //this.vertices.push(new THREE.Vertex(origin));

    for ( i = 0; i < ( iVer + 1 ) ; i++ ) {

        var fRad1 = i / iVer;
        var fRad2 = (i + 1) / iVer;
        var fX1 = innerRadius * Math.cos( fRad1 * twopi );
        var fY1 = innerRadius * Math.sin( fRad1 * twopi );
        var fX2 = outerRadius * Math.cos( fRad1 * twopi );
        var fY2 = outerRadius * Math.sin( fRad1 * twopi );
        var fX4 = innerRadius * Math.cos( fRad2 * twopi );
        var fY4 = innerRadius * Math.sin( fRad2 * twopi );
        var fX3 = outerRadius * Math.cos( fRad2 * twopi );
        var fY3 = outerRadius * Math.sin( fRad2 * twopi );

        var v1 = new THREE.Vector3( fX1, fY1, 0 );
        var v2 = new THREE.Vector3( fX2, fY2, 0 );
        var v3 = new THREE.Vector3( fX3, fY3, 0 );
        var v4 = new THREE.Vector3( fX4, fY4, 0 );
        this.vertices.push( new THREE.Vertex( v1 ) );
        this.vertices.push( new THREE.Vertex( v2 ) );
        this.vertices.push( new THREE.Vertex( v3 ) );
        this.vertices.push( new THREE.Vertex( v4 ) );

    }

    for ( i = 0; i < iVer ; i++ ) {

        this.faces.push(new THREE.Face3( i * 4, i * 4 + 1, i * 4 + 2));
        this.faces.push(new THREE.Face3( i * 4, i * 4 + 2, i * 4 + 3));
        this.faceVertexUvs[ 0 ].push( [
                                new THREE.UV(0, 1),
```

```
                                                      new THREE.UV(1, 1),
                                                      new THREE.UV(1, 0) ] );
            this.faceVertexUvs[ 0 ].push( [
                                                      new THREE.UV(0, 1),
                                                      new THREE.UV(1, 0),
                                                      new THREE.UV(0, 0) ] );
    }

    this.computeCentroids();
    this.computeFaceNormals();

    this.boundingSphere = { radius: outerRadius };
};

Saturn.Rings.prototype = new THREE.Geometry();
Saturn.Rings.prototype.constructor = Saturn.Rings;
```

Saturn.Rings subclasses THREE.Geometry. Its entire job is to create the vertices and faces of our ring geometry. We pass in an inner and outer radius, as well as a number of segments to generate, in order to control the level of resolution. First, we do a little trigonometry to generate vertex positions and push them onto the object's array of vertices. Then, we use that list to create the polygons, or *faces*, of the mesh (in this case, triangles). This defines the shape of our ring. See Figure 3-10 for a wireframe rendering.

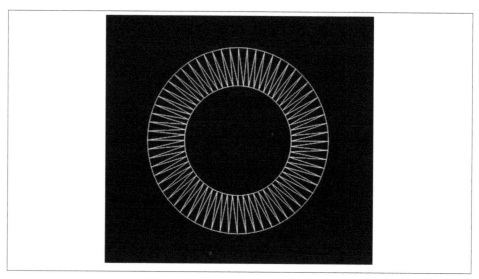

Figure 3-10. Wireframe rendering of ring geometry

In order to properly texture the mesh, we also need to supply Three.js with *texture coordinates*, also known as *UV coordinates*. UV coordinates define the mapping of pixels in a texture to vertices in a face. UV coordinates are typically specified in a space ranging from 0 to 1 horizontally and vertically, with U values increasing to the right and V values increasing upward. In our example, each pair of triangles defines a quad that is going to be textured with the simple map depicted in Figure 3-11. This is a PNG file with some transparency, to give us the effect of the separation visible in some of Saturn's rings. The pixels of this texture are mapped in such a way that the leftmost part of the texture starts at the inside of the ring, and the rightmost part ends at the outer part of the ring.

Figure 3-11. Texture map for Saturn's rings

Once we have set up the vertices, faces, and texture coordinates, we just need to do a little bookkeeping required by all Three.js geometry types. We call upon `computeCent roids()` and set the `boundingSphere` to provide information necessary for picking and culling (topics we'll cover later), and call `computeFaceNormals()` so that Three.js knows how to light the object. Finally, we set the object's `constructor` property so that we are playing nice with the Three.js framework. The final result, a fair approximation of Saturn's familiar rings, is shown in Figure 3-12.

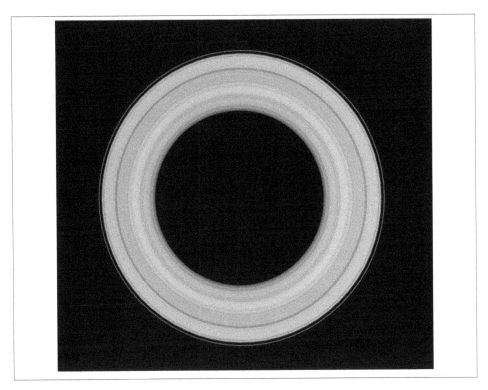

Figure 3-12. Saturn's rings with PNG texture

Rendering Points and Lines

Thus far, all of our talk about rendering has been confined to polygonal meshes, ultimately based on triangles. Triangles are the fundamental rendering primitive available in WebGL, and by far the most commonly used. WebGL eats triangles for breakfast—a good implementation on good hardware can process millions of them per second in real time. But there are two other important primitives available to us: points and lines. We'll make use of both to add a bit of polish to our model.

Point Rendering with Particle Systems

The solar system would look pretty lonely without some stars in the background. So let's create some by rendering points. Three.js has built-in support for WebGL point rendering using its `ParticleSystem` object. In general, particle systems are extremely powerful—they can be used to create effects such as fire, explosions, rain, snow, confetti, and so on. We will be discussing them in more detail in a later chapter. For now, we are going to use a particle system to simply render a static set of points that don't move around on the screen.

A particle system is described by a set of points—Three.js vector objects—that define positions in space, plus a material. The material defines a base color, a size for drawing the point (in pixels), and other optional parameters such as a texture map. We are going to keep it and just draw points with a color and size. Have a look at the listing in Example 3-6 (file *Chapter 3/stars.js*).

Example 3-6. Rendering stars using a particle system (WebGL point primitive)

```
Stars.prototype.init = function(minDistance)
{
    // Create a group to hold our Stars particles
    var starsGroup = new THREE.Object3D();

    var i;
    var starsGeometry = new THREE.Geometry();

    // Create random particle locations
    for ( i = 0; i < Stars.NVERTICES; i++)
    {

        var vector = new THREE.Vector3(
                (Math.random() * 2 - 1) * minDistance,
                (Math.random() * 2 - 1) * minDistance,
                (Math.random() * 2 - 1) * minDistance);

        if (vector.length() <  minDistance)
        {
            vector = vector.setLength(minDistance);
        }
```

```
        starsGeometry.vertices.push( new THREE.Vertex( vector ) );

    }

    // Create a range of sizes and colors for the stars
    var starsMaterials = [];
    for (i = 0; i < Stars.NMATERIALS; i++)
    {
        starsMaterials.push(
                new THREE.ParticleBasicMaterial(
                    { color: 0x101010 * (i + 1),
                    size: i % 2 + 1,
                    sizeAttenuation: false } )
                );
    }

    // Create several particle systems spread around in a circle,
    cover the sky
    for ( i = 0; i < Stars.NPARTICLESYSTEMS; i ++ )
    {

        var stars = new THREE.ParticleSystem( starsGeometry,
            starsMaterials[ i % Stars.NMATERIALS ] );

        stars.rotation.y = i / (Math.PI * 2);

        starsGroup.add( stars );

    }


    // Tell the framework about our object
    this.setObject3D(starsGroup);
}

Stars.NVERTICES = 667;
Stars.NMATERIALS = 8;
Stars.NPARTICLESYSTEMS = 24;
```

First, we create a group to hold the particle systems. Then, we create an empty THREE.Geometry object that is going to be used to hold the vertices we generate for the point locations. Next, we generate several hundred random points, making sure they lie at a minimum distance away from our sun, past Pluto—we don't want any points overlapping our planet geometry and ruining the illusion!

Now, we make a few different materials of type THREE.ParticleBasicMaterial. This object defines the point size and color for the particle system; we want a range of colors (grayscale) and sizes to emulate stars of different magnitude. Note the third parameter, `sizeAttenuation`. By setting it to `false`, we are telling Three.js not to bother trying to resize each particle as the camera moves. We want our stars to look far away no matter what.

Now we are ready to create our `ParticleSystem` objects. We are actually going to create several and spread them around in a circle, picking a random material for each one. We add each particle system to the containing group and we're done. The combination of random sizes and positions and gray/white color values makes for a convincing—if not scientifically accurate—stellar background.

Line Rendering

Orbit lines are a classic feature of solar system illustrations and computer models. In my opinion, no simulation would be complete without them. Happily, Three.js has a built-in line type that does WebGL rendering for us in a snap. Let's look at how it's done. The code listing for file *Chapter 3/orbit.js* can be found in Example 3-7.

Example 3-7. Rendering orbits with lines
```
// Custom Orbit class
Orbit = function()
{
    Sim.Object.call(this);
}

Orbit.prototype = new Sim.Object();

Orbit.prototype.init = function(distance)
{
    // Create an empty geometry object to hold the line vertex data
    var geometry = new THREE.Geometry();

    // Create points along the circumference of a circle
    with radius == distance
    var i, len = 60, twopi = 2 * Math.PI;
    for (i = 0; i <= Orbit.N_SEGMENTS; i++)
    {
        var x = distance * Math.cos( i / Orbit.N_SEGMENTS * twopi );
        var z = distance * Math.sin( i / Orbit.N_SEGMENTS * twopi );
        var vertex = new THREE.Vertex (new THREE.Vector3(x, 0, z));
        geometry.vertices.push(vertex);
    }

    material = new THREE.LineBasicMaterial(
        { color: 0xffffff, opacity: .5, linewidth: 2 } );

    // Create the line
    var line = new THREE.Line( geometry, material );
```

```
    // Tell the framework about our object
    this.setObject3D(line);
}

Orbit.N_SEGMENTS = 120;
```

Our `Orbit` initializer takes a single argument, `distance`, which defines the radius of the orbit. (As a reminder, we're cheating a bit here because planetary orbits are actually elliptical; but a circle will suffice for our needs.) We create an empty geometry object that we are going to populate with line data and then generate vector data for the circumference of a circle in the `x-z` plane (another simplification, rather than dealing with the variations in planetary orbital inclinations). We then create a material suitable for use in rendering lines, `THREE.LineBasicMaterial`. We can specify a thickness for the line, a color, and a transparency value. Now we make the line set, `THREE.Line`, by connecting up the geometry and material object. And that's it.

Writing a Shader

At this point, we've got a pretty nice solar system: beautifully textured planets in animated orbit; distinguishing features like the moon and Saturn's rings; a starry background; and classic orbit lines. We're only missing one thing: a blazing sun. We could take the easy way out here and just put in a big sphere with a texture on it. But we can do better. We are going to make a really awesome, dynamic sun by way of tackling this chapter's final topic: writing a shader.

Shaders can be pretty intimidating at first. They're written in a C-like language, less friendly than JavaScript; they require a lot more math and deeper graphics understanding than anything we have dealt with so far; and when they don't work, at best, things look ugly, and at worst, nothing shows up on the screen at all. In other words: shaders are not for the faint of heart. Well, intrepid reader, it's time to boldly go where few web programmers have gone before.

WebGL Shader Basics

WebGL shaders are based on GLSL ES, the stripped-down version of OpenGL Shading Language (GLSL) used with OpenGL ES. Recall that OpenGL ES is the lightweight version of OpenGL on which WebGL is based. Alphabet soup aside, OpenGL ES is a high-level shading language based on the syntax of the C programming language. C-like constructs are used to write small programs that get compiled into machine code suitable for the target machine's graphics processor (GPU). These programs convert the raw vertex data for meshes, points, and lines into pixels on the screen.

To write a shader, you actually write two programs: a *vertex shader* and a *fragment shader*. A vertex shader, as the name implies, processes vertices. It takes as input a vertex position in 3D space and transforms it into a screen-space pixel position. Once that 2D position has been calculated, the fragment shader is run to calculate the color value of that pixel, including alpha for transparency effects. Note that each vertex and fragment shader pair is executed, in that order, for *every* vertex in a primitive—kind of amazing when you think about it.

Shader programs take different kinds of parameters as input, and the vertex shader can actually generate output parameters that are then passed to the fragment shader. The most common types of shader parameters are:

Attributes
> Components of a single vertex such as position, normal vector, or color that are contained within the vertex buffer data bound to the primitive

Varying parameters
> Parameters whose output values can change for each vertex, for use in the fragment shader; for example, texture coordinates required by the fragment shader

Uniform parameters
> Parameters whose values remain constant for every vertex, such as world transformation and projection matrices

Let's take a quick look again at that shader source code from our trivial shader in Chapter 1, so we can start to get comfortable with the GLSL language. See Example 3-8.

Example 3-8. A very simple WebGL shader
```
var vertexShaderSource =

    "    attribute vec3 vertexPos;\n" +
    "    uniform mat4 modelViewMatrix;\n" +
    "    uniform mat4 projectionMatrix;\n" +
    "    void main(void) {\n" +
    "        // Return the transformed and projected vertex value\n" +
    "        gl_Position = projectionMatrix * modelViewMatrix * \n" +
    "                vec4(vertexPos, 1.0);\n" +
    "    }\n";

var fragmentShaderSource =
    "    void main(void) {\n" +
    "        // Return the pixel color: always output white\n" +
    "        gl_FragColor = vec4(1.0, 1.0, 1.0, 1.0);\n" +
    "}\n";
```

Ignore all the newlines and string concatenation; that's just JavaScript kruft so that we can pass strings to WebGL's shader compiling functions. In this example, we see the GLSL source for two programs: the vertex shader and fragment shader. The vertex shader takes as input a modelViewMatrix, required to convert the mesh from our user-friendly 3D coordinate space into the coordinate space of the camera, and a projectionMatrix, which projects a 3D vertex position into 2D. The two matrices are composed (i.e., multiplied together), and that composed matrix is used to transform the original vertex position, which is passed in as attribute `vertexPos`. In one simple line of code, a lot is going on. GLSL has built-in matrix and vector types, and built-in operators for multiplying them. The result is stored in a GLSL predefined variable called `gl_Position`. The primary job of the vertex shader is to output that value so that the fragment shader can get to work on it.

Now it's the fragment shader's turn. In this trivial example, it simply stores a four-component RGBA white value into a GLSL predefined variable called `gl_FragColor`. In practice, most fragment shaders will use a combination of *uniform* and *varying* inputs such as material colors, vertex normals, texture maps, and texture coordinates to produce the final pixel result.

To actually execute the shader program shown here, you need to plug it into the WebGL pipeline using a variety of functions to compile the GLSL code, bind the various parameters of the shader to objects in your JavaScript code, and set up that shader as the one to use. Once that setup takes place, you draw your primitive. As we have seen, there are a lot of steps to go through if you are using raw WebGL calls, but thankfully, once again it's Three.js to the rescue.

Shaders in Three.js

Have a look at *src/renderers/WebGLRenderer.js* and *src/renderers/WebGLShaders.js* in the Three.js source tree and you will find a set of machinery for handling shader construction and setup. Most shader programs follow common patterns in terms of the attributes and parameters required. For example, vertex shaders rely on a `modelView Matrix` and `projectionMatrix` to transform vertex inputs. Three.js sets up many of these automatically for us so that we can just use them in our shaders. It also has a nice facility for declaring new uniform parameters using a friendly JSON syntax. The bottom line is that you can just focus on writing your shader code and parameter declarations and Three.js will take care of the rest. Let's see how it works.

Our shader-based sun is a swirling fireball. We are going to get this effect by combining a couple of dynamically moving textures: a red-and-yellow color pattern for the base color, and a PNG that will do double-duty, as a source of pseudorandom noise and containing dark and light areas to emulate sunspots. Example 3-9 contains the JavaScript code, from file *Chapter 3/sun-shader.js*.

Example 3-9. Sun object with shader
```
// Custom Sun class
Sun = function()
{
    Sim.Object.call(this);
}

Sun.prototype = new Sim.Object();
```

```
Sun.prototype.init = function()
{

    // Create a group to hold our sun mesh and light
    var sunGroup = new THREE.Object3D();

    var SUNMAP = "./images/lavatile.jpg";
    var NOISEMAP = "./images/cloud.png";
    var uniforms = {

            time: { type: "f", value: 1.0 },
            texture1: { type: "t", value: 0,
                texture: THREE.ImageUtils.loadTexture( NOISEMAP  ) },
            texture2: { type: "t", value: 1,
                texture: THREE.ImageUtils.loadTexture( SUNMAP ) }

        };

    uniforms.texture1.texture.wrapS =
        uniforms.texture1.texture.wrapT = THREE.Repeat;
    uniforms.texture2.texture.wrapS =
        uniforms.texture2.texture.wrapT = THREE.Repeat;

    var material = new THREE.ShaderMaterial( {

        uniforms: uniforms,
        vertexShader:
            document.getElementById( 'vertexShader' ).textContent,
        fragmentShader:
            document.getElementById( 'fragmentShader' ).textContent

    } );

    // Create our sun mesh
    var geometry = new THREE.SphereGeometry(Sun.SIZE_IN_EARTHS, 64, 64);
    sunMesh = new THREE.Mesh( geometry, material );

    // Tuck away the uniforms so that we can animate them over time
    this.uniforms = uniforms;

    // Set up a clock to drive the animation
    this.clock = new THREE.Clock();

    // Create a point light to show off our solar system
    var light = new THREE.PointLight( 0xffffff, 1.2, 100000 );

    sunGroup.add(sunMesh);
    sunGroup.add(light);

    // Tell the framework about our object
    this.setObject3D(sunGroup);
}
```

```
Sun.prototype.update = function()
{
    var delta = this.clock.getDelta();

     this.uniforms.time.value += delta;

    Sim.Object.prototype.update.call(this);

    this.object3D.rotation.y -= 0.001;
}

Sun.SIZE_IN_EARTHS = 100;
```

The first bit of shader work comes in declaring the custom uniform parameters. We declare a local variable, uniforms, to hold the declarations. There are three uniforms: a time value that will drive the dynamic texture animation, and the two textures. Each parameter has a name, which is the property name of the JavaScript object (time, texture1, texture2). Each property has an associated object that describes type and initial value information. In the case of the time uniform, value is just a floating-point number (JavaScript Number type). For the textures, we declare value to be a unique index for that texture, and pass the texture information in the texture property as a Three.js texture object. Under the covers, Three.js will translate this all into raw WebGL data structures to pass to the shader when setting it up.

From here, we create a Three.js material to use all this information. Once again we will use THREE.ShaderMaterial, the type we used in our normal-mapped Earth example earlier in this chapter. Only this time, we are going to provide the shader code ourselves, not use one of the canned types from the shader utility library. We do this by providing the source text to both the vertex and fragment shaders.

There is one more step to wire up the JavaScript for this particular shader. Because we are going to animate the textures to get a swirling effect, we need to pass dynamic values through the uniform parameters. We tuck away the uniform data into our Sun object, and then in our update() method, we change the time value. We are using a Three.js utility object, Clock, to measure our time values. This is basically just a wrapper around built-in JavaScript Date methods, but it comes in handy for driving time-based animations. We are going to talk a lot more about time-based animations in the next chapter. As a final flourish, update() also rotates our sun very slowly about the y-axis.

That's it for the JavaScript part. Now on to the real work: the shader. Example 3-10 shows a portion of the containing HTML page, which includes blobs of GLSL ES source code embedded as script tags.

Example 3-10. Sun shader GLSL ES source code

```
<script id="fragmentShader" type="x-shader/x-fragment">

    uniform float time;

    uniform sampler2D texture1;
    uniform sampler2D texture2;

    varying vec2 texCoord;

    void main( void ) {

        vec4 noise = texture2D( texture1, texCoord );

        vec2 T1 = texCoord + vec2( 1.5, -1.5 ) * time  * 0.01;
        vec2 T2 = texCoord + vec2( -0.5, 2.0 ) * time *  0.01;

        T1.x -= noise.r * 2.0;
        T1.y += noise.g * 4.0;
        T2.x += noise.g * 0.2;
        T2.y += noise.b * 0.2;

        float p = texture2D( texture1, T1 * 2.0 ).a + 0.25;

        vec4 color = texture2D( texture2, T2 );
        vec4 temp = color * 2.0 * ( vec4( p, p, p, p ) ) +
            ( color * color );
        gl_FragColor = temp;
    }

</script>

<script id="vertexShader" type="x-shader/x-vertex">

    varying vec2 texCoord;

    void main()
    {
        texCoord = uv;
        vec4 mvPosition = modelViewMatrix *
            vec4( position, 1.0 );
        gl_Position = projectionMatrix * mvPosition;
    }

</script>
```

In this example, note how we pass the shader source programs to the application: they have been loaded into the containing page content via putting GLSL source text into <script> tags, so we can just grab the textContent DOM attribute out of it. That's the easiest way to get it done, though of course it has one big drawback: it's not as modular as it could be because you need to include the shader source in markup in the main page. There are alternate ways to do this, such as concatenating strings embedded in the JavaScript (as we saw in the previous example), or loading external shader source files as text via Ajax. This method is just the easiest, so we're going with it. Each script tag has an `id` so that we can retrieve the content using DOM methods. It also indicates a MIME type on this so that the browser knows to treat it as foreign content. The content area of the script contains the actual GLSL source.

Let's look at the vertex shader first. As with our previous example, it's not very radical. It just transforms the model-space 3D coordinates into screen-space pixels. The only new thing here is the varying parameter, `texCoord`. GLSL ES doesn't automatically pass texture coordinates to the fragment shader, and we are going to need those. By copying the value of `uv`, an attribute predefined for us by Three.js in its shader setup code, to `texCoord`, we are able to pass the texture coordinates defined in the sphere mesh to the fragment shader so that it can mess around with them to create the swirling effect.

Now for the fragment shader. This is where the hard work takes place. First let's take a look at the source textures that create the effect. Figure 3-13 shows the color map, a chaotic blend of red and yellow. Figure 3-14 shows the noise and alpha map.

Figure 3-13. Color map for sun shader

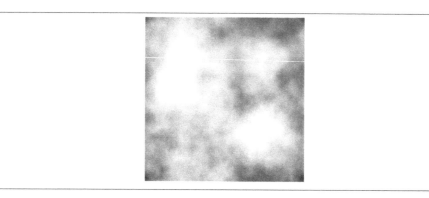

Figure 3-14. Noise/alpha map for sun shader

For the second map, the white areas you see in the screenshot are actually transparent. We are going to use those zero-alpha values as sunspots. The texture also has a fairly random pattern of pixel values that we will use to generate noise.

The fragment shader starts with declarations of the three uniforms, and the varying `texCoord` parameter. Now for the main program: we start by getting our noise value. The `texture2D()` function returns the pixel content in `texture1` at the provided texture coordinate. We then generate additional texture coordinates to index into the noise map again for the alpha value, and into the color map for the base color value. We use the passed-in time (in seconds) as the multiplier for a couple of vectors that offset into the textures at different rates. This is what creates the basic swirling effect. But it's a smooth effect if we stop there. To make the swirling motion truly chaotic, we are going to add noise. We actually use RBG values from the noise texture as vector offsets into the texture coordinate. For the sunspots, we then get an alpha value out of the noise texture, stored in the color's `a` component, for use as a grayscale value in our final color calculation (this technique is an optimization that lets us use a single texture to pass in two kinds of information). We extract the base color from the color map texture, combine it with the alpha-derived grayscale value, and produce our final color. Last, we save this color into the GLSL ES predefined variable `gl_FragColor`. The result: a chaotic, red-and-yellow swirling mass with dark spots moving across it—a.k.a. the sun.

Chapter Summary

In this chapter, we took a grand tour of WebGL graphics features and the powerful Three.js constructs for making them. In building our solar system model, we learned how to create meshes and shade them using materials, textures, and lights, giving our Earth a realistic look; we used the transform hierarchy to create satellites and simple orbit animations; we wrote our own geometry object type to get Saturn's rings just right; and we also learned how to use WebGL point and line rendering to convey more information. Finally, we wrote our first honest-to-goodness GLSL shader to present a dynamic, blazing sun. It was a lot to cover, but it was worth it.

This chapter really only scratched the surface of graphics. There are many types of rendering techniques using multiple textures, beyond the normal mapping we used for our Earth. Particle systems, which we employed in static form for our fake star background, can deliver highly dynamic real-world effects such as fire and precipitation. And the sky is truly the limit when it comes to shader-based programming. Those are just some of the tricks available to us in the WebGL bag. In a later chapter, we will go deeper into graphics, but for now our work here is done.

CHAPTER 4

Animation

If graphics is the heart of WebGL, animation is its soul. With animation, an otherwise static WebGL scene comes to life, making it richer, more informative, and more entertaining. WebGL gives us the ability to render graphics at 60 frames per second; it sure would be a waste of that power if nothing on the screen were moving!

WebGL doesn't have much in the way of built-in animation capability. However, Three.js has some great animation utilities, and we are starting to see other libraries emerge to fill the vacuum. We will have a look at one, Tween.js, in this chapter. If your application is sufficiently complex, you may find the need to build your own animation framework. Given its relative importance in the world of WebGL, we are going to devote a chapter to learning as much as we can about this topic.

We have already seen simple animation in previous chapters, such as spinning cubes, rotating planets, and dancing textures that simulate the sun. Admittedly, we created some nice effects, but most of the animations were done as ad hoc hacks to support learning graphics. In this chapter, we will take a more formal approach to animating our WebGL scenes. Let's start by talking about core concepts.

Animation Basics

Ultimately, animation is about something on the screen changing over time: cars driving, lights blinking, facial expressions changing. These are different effects, achieved through various techniques, but in the end, they all result in making changes to the rendered scene over time.

Frame-Based Animation

Computer-generated animation traces its roots back to film and cartoon cel animation. You are probably aware that a film's moving picture is composed of a series of still images, or *frames*, that, when presented in rapid succession, trick the eye into perceiving a smooth, moving image. In cartoons, a series of transparent overlays, or cels, are placed on a still background to create the illusion of the cel's contents moving against that background. This technique of presenting a succession of discrete frames, tied to a specific fraction of a second in time, is known as *frame-based animation*.

Early computer animation systems emulated this technique from film by presenting a succession of still images on the display, or, in vector-based graphics, a series of vector-based images generated by the program for each frame. Historically, film was shot and played back at a rate of 24 images per second, known as a *frame rate* of 24 frames per second (FPS). This speed was adequate for large projection screens in low light settings. However, in the world of computer-generated animation and 3D games, our senses are actually able to perceive and appreciate changes that occur at higher frame rates, upward of 30 and up to 60 or more FPS. Despite this, many animation systems, such as Adobe Flash, originally adopted the 24 FPS convention due to its familiarity for traditional animators (not to mention having to live with the practical constraints at the time—namely, slow computers that had a hard time actually presenting the images that fast). These days, the frame rates have changed—Flash supports 60 FPS if the developer requests it—but the concept of discrete frames remains.

Time-Based Animation

Frame-based animation has one serious drawback: by tying it to a specific frame rate, the animator has ensured that the animation will never be able to be presented at a higher frame rate, even if the computer can support it. This was no big deal for film, where the hardware was fairly uniform throughout the industry. However, in computer animation, performance can vary wildly from one device to the next. If you create your animations at 24 FPS, but your computer can handle 60, you effectively deprive the user of resolution and smoothness.

Another technique, known as *time-based animation*, solves this problem. In time-based animation, a series of vector graphics images is connected to particular points in time, not specific frames in a sequence with known frame rates. In this way, the computer can present those images and the interpolated frames in between them (see the next section) as frequently as possible and deliver the best images and smoothest transitions. We actually saw an example of time-based animation at work in our shader-based sun in Chapter 3: elapsed time was used as the driving function to change the pixels on the sun's surface. All of the examples developed for this and subsequent chapters use time-based animation.

Interpolation and Tweening

Vector graphics differs fundamentally from bitmapped graphics. Rather than presenting an image on the screen, a program makes calls to a drawing library using primitives such as lines and polygons. Because of this, animators can take advantage of a very powerful animation technique known as *tweening* to save time. Tweening is the process of generating vector values that lie in between a pair of other vector values. With tweening, an animator does not need to supply the vector values of the graphic for each frame; he can supply them, say, every half second or at preferred positions, called *keyframes*, and the computer generates (tweens) the intervening values.

 Bitmap-based tweening is also possible, but its use is very limited to effects such as a morph between two images.

Tweening is accomplished using a mathematical technique called *interpolation*. Interpolation refers to the generation of a value that lies between two values, based on a scalar value input such as a time or fraction value. Interpolation is illustrated in Figure 4-1. For any values A and B, and a fraction u between 0 and 1, the interpolated value P can be calculated by the formula A + u * (B-A). This is the simplest form of interpolation, known as *linear interpolation* because the mathematical function used to calculate the result could be graphed with a straight line. Other, more complex interpolation functions, such as splines (a type of curve) and polynomials, are also used in animation systems.

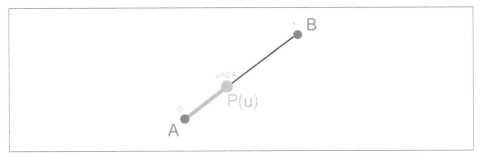

Figure 4-1. Linear interpolation (available at http://content.gpwiki.org/images/0/06/ Linear_interlopation_diagram.png)

In 3D animation, interpolation is used to calculate tweens of 3D positions, rotations, colors, scalar values (such as transparency), and more. With a multicomponent value such as a 3D vector, a linearly interpolated tween simply interpolates each component piecewise. For example, the interpolated value P at u=0.5 for the 3D vector AB from (0, 0, 0) to (1, 2, 3) would be (0.5, 1, 1.5).

Keyframes

A very simple animation, such as moving an object from one point on the screen to another, can be achieved by specifying the two end points and a time duration. Over that duration, u values are continually recalculated as a fraction between 0 and 1 (elapsed time, divided by the duration) and the resultant tween computed as an interpolation based on u.

More complex animations take the tween concept to the next level, using *keyframes*. Rather than specifying a single pair of values to tween, a keyframe animation consists of a list of values, with potentially different durations in between each successive value. Example 4-1 shows sample keyframe values for an animation that move an object from the origin up and away from the camera. Over the course of one second, the object moves upward in the first quarter of a second, then up some more and away from the camera in the remaining three-quarters of a second. The animation system will calculate tweens for the points (0, 0, 0) to (0, 1, 0) over the first quarter second, then tweens for (0, 1, 0) to (0, 2, 5) over the remaining three quarters of a second. Keyframe animations can work with linear interpolation, or more complex interpolation such as spline-based; the data points representing the keys can be treated as points in a line graph or as the graph of a more complicated function such as a cubic spline.

Example 4-1. Sample keyframe data
```
var keys = [0, 0.25, 1];
var values = [new THREE.Vector3(0, 0, 0),
    new THREE.Vector3(0, 1, 0),
    new THREE.Vector3(0, 2, 5)];
```

Note that the term *keyframe animation* is used in both frame-based and time-based systems—a holdover from frame-based nomenclature. Keyframing works equally well in both types of animation system.

Articulated Animation

The animation strategies we have discussed so far can be used to move simple objects in place (i.e., with rotation) or around the screen, and they can also be used to create complex motions in composite objects using a transform hierarchy. We saw this in play in the preceding chapter in the solar system model as the Earth moved in orbit around the sun, and the moon around the Earth. Watch the model in action, and you will see the moon trace a rather complicated path around the sun. This is the net effect of individually animating the combined transforms.

In the case of the solar system, the moon's eccentric path around the sun is a bit of an accident, the natural outcome of the hierarchy of celestial bodies. But we can take advantage of this same capability to create an intentional effect in our animations. Let's say we want to create a robot that walks and waves its arms. We would model the robot as a hierarchical structure: the robot body contains an upper body and lower body, the upper body contains arms and a torso, the arms contain upper arms and lower arms, and so on. By properly constructing the hierarchy and animating the right parts, we can get the robot to moves its arms and legs. We will do just that later in this chapter. The technique of constructing bodies by combining a hierarchy of discrete parts and animating them in combinations is known as *articulated animation*.

Skinned Animation

Articulated animation works very well for inorganic objects—robots, cars, machines, and so on. It breaks down badly for organic objects. Plants swaying in the breeze, animals bounding, and people dancing all involve changes to the geometry of a mesh—for example, skin ripples, muscles bulge. It is nearly impossible to do this well with the Tinkertoy approach that is articulated animation. So we turn to another technique called *skinned animation*, or *single mesh animation*.

Skinned animation involves deforming the actual vertices of a mesh, or *skin*, over time. There is still a hierarchy underlying the animation, known as a *skeleton*. It is like the body of the robot, but it is only used as the underlying mechanism for animating; we don't see it on the screen. Changes to the skeleton, combined with additional data describing how the skeleton influences changes to the skin in various regions of the mesh, drive the skinned animation. We will demonstrate an example of a skinned animation in a later chapter.

Morphs

We have one final animation concept to cover briefly before we get our hands dirty: *morph target animation*, or simply, *morphing*. Morphing involves vertex-based interpolations used to change the vertices of a mesh. Typically, a subset of the vertices of a mesh is stored, along with their indices, as a set of *morph targets* to be used in a tween. The tween interpolates between each of the vertex values in the morph targets, and the animation uses the interpolated values to deform the vertices in the mesh. Morph targets are excellent for facial expressions and other fine details that are not so easy to implement in a skinned animation; they are quite compact and don't require a highly detailed skeleton with numerous facial bones.

In addition, they allow the animator to create very specific expressions by tweaking the mesh right down to the vertex level. Figure 4-2 illustrates the use of morphing to create facial expressions. Each different expression, such as the pursed lips or the smile, is represented by a set of vertices including the mouth and surrounding areas.

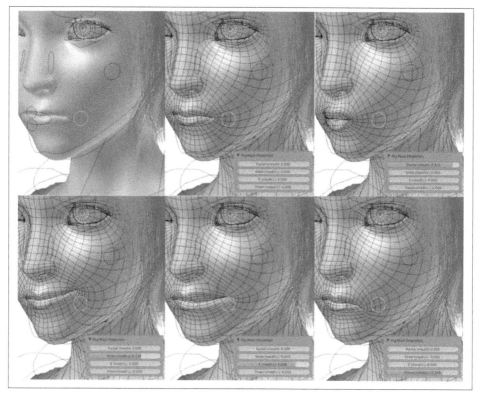

Figure 4-2. Facial morphs (http://en.wikipedia.org/wiki/File:Sintel-face-morph.png, Creative Commons Attribution-Share Alike 3.0 Unported license)

Creating Tweens Using the Tween.js Library

It's pretty straightforward to implement a basic animation engine on your own. Still, there are a lot of details to get right, especially if you want to have nonlinear interpolation functions, and bells and whistles like ease in/ease out, where the animation appears to accelerate to its main speed and decelerate out of it. Tween.js, an open source tweening library created by Soledad Penadés (*https://github.com/sole*), is gaining popularity in web development, particularly for use with the Three.js tookit.

Tween.js is really handy for quickly building simple tweens with ease in/out functionality. I personally find that it breaks down for use in complex animations. But it's a great place to get started. Let's build our first animations using Tween.js. Go get the latest GitHub repository at *https://github.com/sole/tween.js* and we'll get going.

Creating a Basic Tween

Figures 4-3 and 4-4 show before-and-after screenshots of our first animation. Open the example file *Chapter 4/tween-basic.html*, and click in the content area to run the animation. You should see the ball move slowly from the left side of the page to the right. Click again and it will move slowly back to the left.

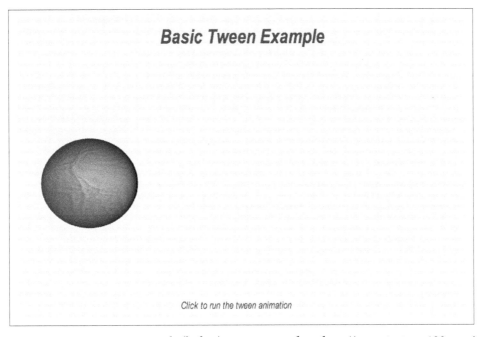

Figure 4-3. Basic tween example (before); texture map from http://www.textures123.com/ free/game-texture.html

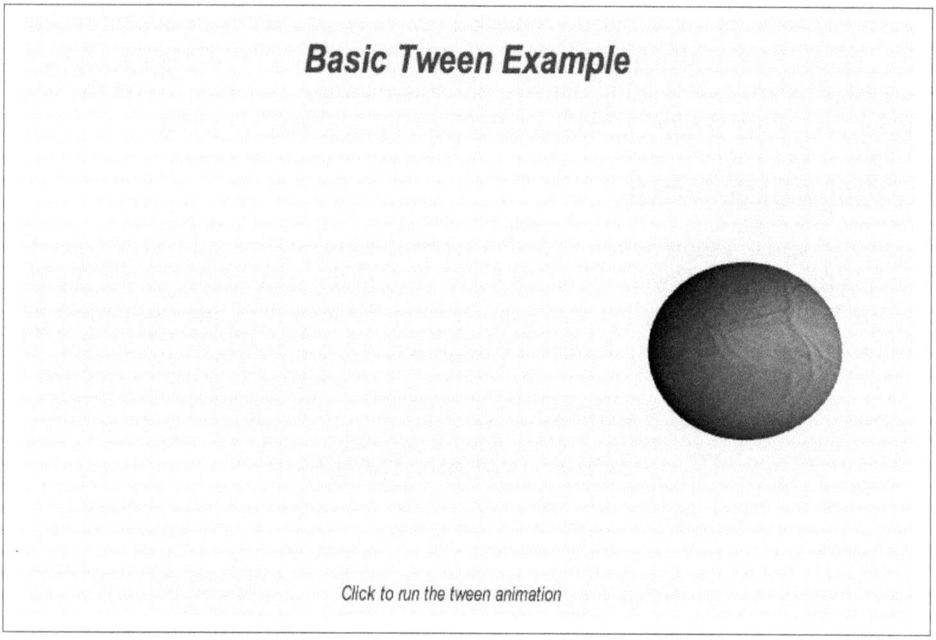

Basic Tween Example

Click to run the tween animation

Figure 4-4. Basic tween example (after)

The code for this page is listed in Example 4-2, and the JavaScript implementation can be found in file *Chapter 4/tween-basic.js*.

Example 4-2. Basic tween example using Tween.js

```
...
// Our custom initializer
TweenApp.prototype.init = function(param)
{
    // Call superclass init code to set up scene, renderer,
    default camera
    Sim.App.prototype.init.call(this, param);

    // Create a point light to show off the MovingBall
    var light = new THREE.PointLight( 0xffffff, 1, 100);
    light.position.set(0, 0, 20);
    this.scene.add(light);

    this.camera.position.z = 6.667;

    // Create the MovingBall and add it to our sim
    var movingBall = new MovingBall();
    movingBall.init();
    this.addObject(movingBall);

    this.movingBall = movingBall;
}
```

```
TweenApp.prototype.update = function()
{
    TWEEN.update();

    Sim.App.prototype.update.call(this);

}

TweenApp.prototype.handleMouseUp = function(x, y)
{
    this.movingBall.animate();
}

// Custom MovingBall class
MovingBall = function()
{
    Sim.Object.call(this);
}

MovingBall.prototype = new Sim.Object();

MovingBall.prototype.init = function()
{
    // Create our MovingBall
    var BALL_TEXTURE = "../images/ball_texture.jpg";
    var geometry = new THREE.SphereGeometry(1, 32, 32);
    var material = new THREE.MeshPhongMaterial(
            { map: THREE.ImageUtils.loadTexture(BALL_TEXTURE) } );
    var mesh = new THREE.Mesh( geometry, material );
    mesh.position.x = -3.333;

    // Tell the framework about our object
    this.setObject3D(mesh);
}

MovingBall.prototype.animate = function()
{
    var newpos;
    if (this.object3D.position.x > 0)
    {
        newpos = this.object3D.position.x - 6.667;
    }
    else
    {
        newpos = this.object3D.position.x + 6.667;
    }

    new TWEEN.Tween(this.object3D.position)
```

```
    .to( {
        x: newpos
    }, 2000).start();
}
```

Continuing with our use of Sim.js (introduced in the preceding chapter), we create an application object, TweenApp. We'll skip over the usual object framing and go right to TweenApp.init(). It creates a light, positions the camera for viewing, and then creates an object of type MovingBall (subclass of Sim.Object). MovingBall is where most of the action is going to take place. But note one more thing about TweenApp: it calls the Tween.js update function, TWEEN.update(), every frame. TWEEN.update() goes through its current list of active animations, updating each one. If we don't call this function, we won't see any animations.

On to MovingBall: the fun here is in the animate() method. First, we apply a little logic to obtain an end position for the animation. If the ball is on the left side, the end position will be on the right, and vice versa. Then we create the tween (code highlighted in bold) and run the animation. Over the course of two seconds, the ball will move smoothly across the screen.

There are actually three things going on here: (1) we create a new TWEEN.Tween object, passing in the target object to animate (i.e., the mesh's position vector); (2) we call its to() method, which sets the target parameters of the animation—in this case, this will animate this.object3D.position.x (ah...the magic of JavaScript property introspection!) over two seconds; and (3) we call the tween object's start() method, to start the animation. One subtlety here is that TWEEN.Tween.to() returns this, allowing methods to be chained, in the style of jQuery. So, in one compact line of code we have created the tween, connected it to our target object, set the target animation parameters, and fired up the animation. Pretty cool.

Tweens with Easing

Our preceding example showed the basics of tweening with Tween.js, but it felt a little flat. The ball moved from one side of the screen to another at a constant rate, with no dynamic changes. It worked, but it didn't feel very natural. We can make more compelling animations by incorporating *easing*—nonlinear functions applied to the start and end of the animation that make it appear to accelerate to its main speed and decelerate out of it.

Run the example depicted in Figure 4-5. See how the ball moves downward at a constant speed initially, then slows down and lands softly at the bottom. Click again; see it move up slowly and then pick up speed to the top. The downward animation is an example of an *ease out* effect, the upward an example of *ease in*.

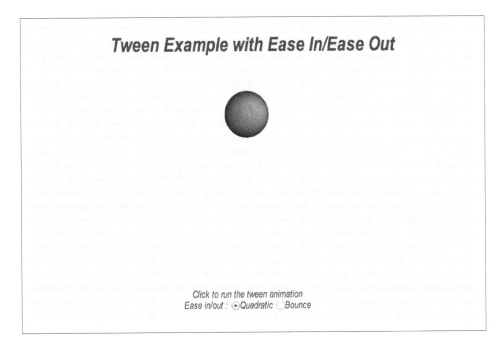

Figure 4-5. Tweens with easing

Now click on the radio button labeled Bounce. This will tell the application to use a different style of easing. Click on the content area and watch the ball bounce as it hits the bottom; click again and the ball will bounce its way up. We are still using ease out on the way down—the ball starts at a constant speed, then seems to speed up, then finally bounces a few times—and ease in on the way up. But this time we are applying a different *easing function*. Let's have a look at an excerpt from the code (see Example 4-3).

Example 4-3. Using Tween.js easing functions
```
MovingBall.prototype.animate = function()
{
    var newpos, easefn;
    if (this.object3D.position.y > 0)
    {
        newpos = this.object3D.position.y - 6.667;
        easefn = MovingBall.useBounceFunction ?
                TWEEN.Easing.Bounce.EaseOut :
                TWEEN.Easing.Quadratic.EaseOut;
    }
    else
    {
        newpos = this.object3D.position.y + 6.667;
        easefn = MovingBall.useBounceFunction ?
                TWEEN.Easing.Bounce.EaseIn :
                TWEEN.Easing.Quadratic.EaseIn;
    }
```

```
new TWEEN.Tween(this.object3D.position)
.to( {
    y: newpos
}, 2000)
.easing(easefn).start();

}

MovingBall.useBounceFunction = false;
```

From the preceding example, we have modified `MovingBall.animate()` and added a static variable, `useBounceFunction`, which flags whether to use the bounce easing functions. `animate()` now contains additional logic to determine which Tween.js easing functions to use. `TWEEN.Easing.Bounce.EaseOut` and the other similarly named easing functions are just that: JavaScript functions. Under the covers, Tween.js applies the easing function to the time value, effectively slowing, speeding up, stopping, and/or reversing time before passing it to the tweening evaluator. Once again, the function calls are chained together, because each one returns `this`, making for a compact coding style.

 The Tween.js easing functions are based on the ActionScript animation work of Robert Penner (*http://www.robertpenner.com/index2.html*). They offer a wide range of powerful easing equations, including linear, quadratic, quartic, sinusoidal, and exponential. Mr. Penner has created a handy page for trying them out using a simple 2D animation, *http:// gizma.com/easing/*. Experiment with them and see what kind of effects you can achieve. These equations have also now been incorporated into the popular jQuery `animate()` function.

Easing is a great tool for adding a more realistic look to your tween animations. It can even do a fair job approximating physics—such as in our bouncing ball example—without the hard work and computational overhead of adding a physics engine to your application. I have also discovered that, combined with interaction, easing can provide for a much more organic and intuitive user experience. By connecting ease in/out tweens to input actions, you can create iOS-style drag and swipe behaviors that feel almost physical, with apparent inertia, momentum, and other lifelike qualities. We'll be talking about this in the next chapter.

As we have just seen, tweens can be great for quickly creating simple effects. Tween.js actually lets you chain animations together into a sequence so that you can compose simple effects into more powerful ones. However, as you begin building complex animation sequences you are going to want a more general solution. With that in mind, we take leave of Tween.js and move on to creating animations based on a keyframe system.

Animating an Articulated Model with Keyframes

Articulated animations move objects by moving their transforms (i.e., positioning and rotating them). Typically not just one transform is animated, but several are animated in a hierarchy. There is no more fun example of articulated animation in action than a robot, so let's animate one. Figure 4-6 depicts a cartoon bot, ready for action.

Figure 4-6. Articulated animation using keyframes; model by 3DBS, http://www.turbosquid.com/FullPreview/Index.cfm/ID/475463

Launch the file *Chapter 4/keyframe-robot.html* to see the robot go. He rotates automatically on page load so that we can get a good look at him from all sides. Click on the content area to start the animation and you will see him go through a walk cycle: the legs alternate taking steps; the body rocks back and forth; the head bobs; the wind-up key rotates. Let's get into the code to see how it's done.

Loading the Model

Thus far, I have been steering clear of talking about modeling formats, because we are going to devote the better part of a chapter to the subject later on. However, at this point, we really need to get into it; otherwise, we would have to build the robot's appearance by hand, programming cubes, cylinders, and such…and the results would be less than pretty. So, I decided to buy a model from TurboSquid (*http://www.turbosquid.com*), a leading 3D art site. TurboSquid offers models in several different file formats, at a wide range of prices, including free. I purchased a "cartoon robot" in the COLLADA file format, an open format defined by the Khronos Group (the same folks who brought us WebGL).

After the usual setup code, we create a new Robot class to implement the robot. First up, we load the model. The excerpt listed in Example 4-4 (file *Chapter 4/keyframe-robot.js*) shows the code to load the model.

Example 4-4. Loading the robot model

```
Robot.prototype.init = function()
{
    // Create a group to hold the robot
    var bodygroup = new THREE.Object3D;
    // Tell the framework about our object
    this.setObject3D(bodygroup);

    var that = this;
    // GREAT cartoon robot model -
    http://www.turbosquid.com/FullPreview/Index.cfm/ID/475463
    // Licensed
    var url = '../models/robot_cartoon_02/robot_cartoon_02.dae';
    var loader = new Sim.ColladaLoader;
    loader.load(url, function (data) {
        that.handleLoaded(data)
    });
}

Robot.prototype.handleLoaded = function(data)
{
    if (data)
    {
        var model = data.scene;
        // This model in cm, we're working in meters, scale down
        model.scale.set(.01, .01, .01);

        this.object3D.add(model);

        // Walk through model looking for known named parts
        var that = this;
        THREE.SceneUtils.traverseHierarchy(model,
            function (n) { that.traverseCallback(n); });

        this.createAnimation();
    }
}

Robot.prototype.traverseCallback = function(n)
{
    // Function to find the parts we need to animate. C'est facile!
    switch (n.name)
```

```
    {
        case 'jambe_G' :
            this.left_leg = n;
            break;
        case 'jambe_D' :
            this.right_leg = n;
            break;
        case 'head_container' :
            this.head = n;
            break;
        case 'clef' :
            this.key = n;
            break;
        default :
            break;
    }
}
```

Our Robot class uses a helper object, `Sim.ColladaLoader`, to load the COLLADA model file located in *models/robot_cartoon_02/robot_cartoon_02.dae*. (This class is actually a modified version of the Three.js COLLADA file loader code, adapted to work around a few issues.) We provide a callback function so that the loader can notify us when the file has been downloaded and parsed. The callback, `handleLoaded()`, grabs the content from `data.scene`, saves it into a local variable `model`, and scales the model to meter-sized units, because it was modeled in centimeters. We know this by inspecting the COLLADA file. Open it with a text editor and look at line 9:

```
<unit meter="0.01" name="centimeter"/>
```

We then insert the model into the scene by adding it as a child of our main group. Before we can animate the model, we need to do one more thing: get access to certain children of the top-level model group in order to animate them. The Three.js utility function `THREE.SceneUtils.traverseHierarchy()` lets us iterate through the object hierarchy to find what we need. In this case, I had to dust off my college French (presumably the native tongue of the artist) to find the legs, head, and wind-up key. Note the one English name: that was something I had to actually add to the model to group all the objects for the head together so that they would animate as a group. With that done, we are now ready to animate the model.

Animating the Model

Three.js comes with built-in animation support. Have a look at the sources under the Three.js tree in *src/extras/animation* and get familiar with the utilities. They are general and powerful—but at the same time I personally find them overkill when it comes to simple keyframing. To explore the basics of keyframe animation, we are going to instead use my own homegrown objects from the Sim.js library.

Our HTML file includes the script *sim/animation.js*, which defines two classes. Sim.Key FrameAnimator is responsible for running an animation containing one or more interpolators. It contains methods to start, stop, and run the animation, a duration parameter, and a loop flag so that you can make the animation run indefinitely. The animation is run out of the animator's update() method, which loops through its list of interpolators to perform a time-based interpolation.

Sim.Interpolator contains a list of keys and values. As with Tween.js, the values are objects that can contain anything: a scalar, a position value, a rotation value, or whatever you like (just make sure the objects' properties have the same names in every value object). The interp() method performs the interpolation, calling its helper method tween() as needed. Sim.Interpolator also takes a target parameter (i.e., an object to copy the interpolated values into). Currently, Sim.Interpolator implements only simple linear interpolation.

Example 4-5 shows the code to set up the animation. We create a new Sim.Key FrameAnimator, initializing it with our interpolator keys and values. Under the covers, the constructor will create instances of Sim.Interpolator objects, one for each entry in the interps array. We set loop to true so that the animation will go on indefinitely (or until we explicitly call stop()). Finally we set the duration to a predefined constant value (in this case, just over one second). Once that value is reached, the animation will resume from the beginning automatically, creating the loop.

Example 4-5. Creating the animation

```
Robot.prototype.createAnimation = function()
{
    this.animator = new Sim.KeyFrameAnimator;
    this.animator.init({
        interps:
            [
                { keys:Robot.bodyRotationKeys,
                    values:Robot.bodyRotationValues,
                    target:this.object3D.rotation },
                { keys:Robot.headRotationKeys,
                    values:Robot.headRotationValues,
                    target:this.head.rotation },
                { keys:Robot.keyRotationKeys,
                    values:Robot.keyRotationValues,
                    target:this.key.rotation },
                { keys:Robot.leftLegRotationKeys,
values:Robot.leftLegRotationValues, target:this.left_leg.rotation },
                { keys:Robot.rightLegRotationKeys,
values:Robot.rightLegRotationValues, target:this.right_leg.rotation },
            ],
        loop: true,
        duration:RobotApp.animation_time
    });
```

```
    this.animator.subscribe("complete", this, this.onAnimationComplete);

    this.addChild(this.animator);
}
```

Now let's look at the interpolator data, shown in Example 4-6. This is defined as a set of properties of the Robot class.

Example 4-6. Keyframe interpolator data
```
Robot.headRotationKeys = [0, .25, .5, .75, 1];
Robot.headRotationValues = [ { z: 0 },
                             { z: -Math.PI / 96 },
                             { z: 0 },
                             { z: Math.PI / 96 },
                             { z: 0 },
                             ];

Robot.bodyRotationKeys = [0, .25, .5, .75, 1];
Robot.bodyRotationValues = [ { x: 0 },
                             { x: -Math.PI / 48 },
                             { x: 0 },
                             { x: Math.PI / 48 },
                             { x: 0 },
                             ];

Robot.keyRotationKeys = [0, .25, .5, .75, 1];
Robot.keyRotationValues = [ { x: 0 },
                            { x: Math.PI / 4 },
                            { x: Math.PI / 2 },
                            { x: Math.PI * 3 / 4 },
                            { x: Math.PI },
                            ];

Robot.leftLegRotationKeys = [0, .25, .5, .75, 1];
Robot.leftLegRotationValues = [ { z: 0 },
                                { z: Math.PI / 6},
                                { z: 0 },
                                { z: 0 },
                                { z: 0 },
                                ];

Robot.rightLegRotationKeys = [0, .25, .5, .75, 1];
Robot.rightLegRotationValues = [ { z: 0 },
                                 { z: 0 },
                                 { z: 0 },
                                 { z: Math.PI / 6},
                                 { z: 0 },
                                 ];
```

Note the numeric values for each array of keys. `Sim.Interpolator.interp()` takes fractional values as input. The time values generated by `Sim.KeyFrameAnimator`'s update method are normalized to the interval [0..1], based on the passed-in duration value: in other words, 0 is the start time of the animation, 1 the end time (or end of a loop cycle, if loop is set to true), regardless of the actual duration of the animation. In this way, we can change the duration of the animation without having to recode all the keys.

In this example, we use five keys for each interpolator, slicing the time interval (cycle) equally into quarters. There is nothing that forces us to use the same number of keys, or the same numeric values for the keys; each set can be different. It just so happens that in this example we want most things to happen at half- and quarter-cycle intervals, so our keys are all the same. The head bobs forward and then back to center over half a cycle, then backward and to center over the second half cycle. The legs alternate moving forward and back by staggering their rotations: the leg left moves from resting rotation to forward over the first quarter cycle, then back to resting at the half cycle; the right leg waits until the half cycle to rotate forward and back. The key simply rotates smoothly in a circle. Finally, the entire body bobs first to the right, then to the left, as the legs move.

This example illustrates the power of the transform hierarchy working in concert with keyframes to create the articulated animation. Transforming an object transforms its descendants, too: rotating the top-level object3D rotates the entire robot model; rotating a leg rotates the foot along with it; rotating the head group moves the entire head.

 You may have noticed that the x- and z-axes for the rotation values are flipped from what you would expect. I can only assume that the artist originally built this model for still renders, not articulated animation. But with a simple x-y swap we have made it work.

That's it for our articulated animation example, and we have still only scratched the surface of using keyframes. Keyframes don't have to use simple linear interpolation; they can employ more powerful types that use nonlinear tweens and easing. In addition to rotations, they can be used to animate position, scale, scalar values (colors, light intensities, etc.), 2D transforms for textures, and more. We will see some of these capabilities in action as we explore how to animate materials, lights, and textures.

Animating Materials and Lights

Animation is really about making changes to the pixels on the screen over time. Those changes don't have to be confined to the transform hierarchy; we can also animate materials and lights to create cool effects.

Most Three.js objects are dynamic in nature: if you change a property such as a position or rotation, you will see that change in the next rendered frame. This is true of materials and lights: changes to the transparency or color value of a material, or the color or intensity of a light, will take immediate effect. Let's combine this idea with keyframe animation and have some fun.

Launch the file *Chapter 4/keyframe-material.html* and you will see a simple scene with a grid floor and some primitives. Each primitive demonstrates animating a different material property: the red sphere's opacity, the blue cube's color, and the yellow cylinder's specular highlights. Click the checkboxes to turn these features on and off. Figure 4-7 shows a screenshot.

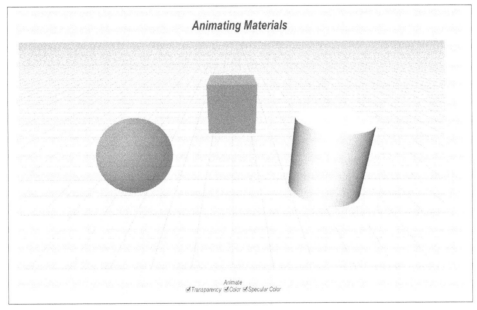

Figure 4-7. Animating opacity, color, and specular highlights

The code for doing this is really simple: just a set of keyframes targeting the respective material properties. Example 4-7 shows the interpolation data for animating the cube's color.

Example 4-7. Interpolation data for animating colors
```
this.colorAnimator = new Sim.KeyFrameAnimator;
this.colorAnimator.init({
    interps:
        [
            {
                keys:[0, .5, 1],
                values:[
```

```
            { r : 0, g : .333, b : 1 },
            { r : 0, g : 1, b : .333 },
            { r : 0, g : .333, b : 1 },
            ],
        target:this.cubematerial.color
    },
    ],
loop: true,
duration:MaterialApp.animation_time
});
```

The preceding keyframes animate the cube color from mostly blue to mostly green; pretty basic stuff. Now, this example is contrived, but imagine the following real-world example: you are building a data visualization program where you want to highlight significant data. By animating color, you can quite easily create blinking and glowing effects for that data, without needing to write shaders or use textures. Material animation is a simple yet very powerful weapon in the WebGL arsenal.

 Our color animation here uses linear interpolation of the red, green, and blue components of an RGB color. This works very well in this particular case, but RGB interpolation in general can be problematic. Many systems offer color interpolation in other spaces, such as HSV. The RGB values are converted to HSV space, the interpolation is performed, and the result is converted back to RGB. You may require this level of sophistication in your work. Luckily, Three.js has utilities to convert to different color spaces. See the files *src/core/Color.js* and *src/extras/ColorUtils.js*.

Animating lights is just as simple as animating materials. Three.js allows you to change intensity, color, and distance properties on the fly. Let's look at an example of animating basic light properties. Launch the file *Chapter 4/keyframe-lights.html*. You will see a highly realistic textured bust of a human male, slowly rotating (see Figure 4-8). Play with the checkboxes at the bottom of the page to see the different effects of animating various light properties.

Lights are a great way to add mood to a scene. By animating them, you can convey time of day, place, and emotional state. Recall that lights also have position and other properties for creating movement. Taken together, these features offer a wide range of possibilities for enhancing games and creating cinematic effects in your web pages.

Animating Textures

We still have to talk about one more tool in our animation palette: textures. Texture animation can make a WebGL scene really "hot" with lots of moving pixels, and convey

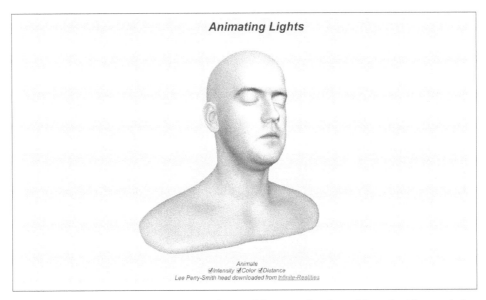

Figure 4-8. Animating light intensity, color, and distance; head model used with permission from Infinite-Realities (http://www.ir-ltd.net/)

a vast amount of dynamic information. Imagine a moving theater marquee, Times Square style, and you'll get the picture. Texture animation can also provide quick-and-dirty effects that would otherwise require computationally expensive vertex manipulation, or labor-intensive shader writing.

Our sun model was essentially a texture animation, since the pixels on the surface of the object were moving. A shader-based texture is also known as a *procedural texture*, because the surface pixels of the object are calculated in code. Procedural textures don't have to be written in a shader; later on in the book, we will see how they can be written with JavaScript code and the Canvas API. But before we get into procedural textures, let's talk about a much simpler way to animate textures using *texture transforms*.

A texture transform, as the name implies, uses a transformation (position and scale) on the texture. In this case, it is a 2D transformation. Using a texture transform, we can offset the pixels in the texture in x and y, and we can scale them such that we are zoomed in on the texture, or zoomed out. Combine this with keyframe animation and you have some inexpensive power at your fingertips. Let's look at an example.

Figure 4-9 shows the texture animation implemented in file *Chapter 4/keyframe-texture.html*. Launch the file, and click in the content area to start and stop the animation. You will see a waterfall against a rock face. The waterfall effect is achieved by simply animating the y offset of the texture map, essentially transforming the position of the texture's UV coordinates. This is one of those "cheap cinematic tricks" you have seen in many 3D games but probably didn't realize that it was just a 2D animation hack. (Pay no attention to that man behind the curtain!) Let's see how it's done.

Figure 4-9. Waterfall using an animated texture; water texture by Patrick Hoesly (http://www.flickr.com/photos/zooboing/4441454031/sizes/o/in/photostream/), attribution 2.0 Generic (CC BY 2.0); rock texture created using FilterForge (http://filterforge.com/), license required for commercial use in your own projects

Example 4-8 shows the code fragment for animating the texture transform. THREE.Tex ture has an offset property, which defines the 2D positional transform to be applied to the texture's UV coordinates. offset is a 2D vector with x and y coordinates; these are automatically added to the current UV coordinates for each vertex by the built-in code for most Three.js shaders; all you need to do is set them. In this example, our interpolator simply animates y values from 1 (the default) to 0, making the water in the texture appear to fall downward.

Example 4-8. Animating a texture transform in Three.js

```
this.animator = new Sim.KeyFrameAnimator;
this.animator.init({
    interps:
        [
            {
                keys:[0, 1],
                values:[
```

```
                          { y: 1},
                          { y: 0},
                          ],
                  target:this.texture.offset
              },
          ],
      loop: true,
      duration:Waterfall.animation_time
});
```

One more thing: we need to make sure that the texture map's wrapping mode is set so that bits wrap around once we have gone outside the regular UV space, instead of falling off the edge of the texture. We do this with the following line of code:

```
map.wrapS = map.wrapT = true;
```

Animating Skinned Meshes and Morphs

Before we conclude our look at animation, I want to touch briefly on skinning and morphs. These are more in-depth topics, involving the tools pipeline, and as such we are not going to dive into writing our own examples here. Instead, I will point you to the Three.js sample files; there are several great skinning and morph examples. Also, have a look at the source code for the Three.js animation utilities under *src/extras/animation*. *Animation.js* and its counterparts implement a rich system that supports keyframe animation with several types of interpolation, as well as skinning and morph targets. Have fun with it!

Chapter Summary

In this chapter, we took a close look at animating WebGL content. Tween.js is a great utility for creating simple one-shot tween effects, and combining those into more complex tween sequences. We used a more general keyframing technique based on the Sim.js utilities to animate an articulated model, a robot with many moving parts. We also explored how to use keyframes to animate materials, lights, and textures to achieve a broad range of effects. As you ramp up your WebGL development, your animation work will likely include all of these tools, as well as skinning and morphs using Three.js.

CHAPTER 5

Interaction

Like any online medium, WebGL is a tripod that stands on three legs: graphics, animation, and *interaction*. Our examples thus far have made very limited use of interaction. We handled mouse clicks in the canvas to toggle animation states; we used controls on the web page to change behaviors in the WebGL scene. But we can go way beyond this. We can click and drag on items in the scene itself, triggering other behaviors. We can also navigate within the scene by manipulating the camera. Furthermore, we can combine these capabilities with animated tweens to give our interactivity a rich, organic feel.

As an experienced web developer, you probably take interaction for granted. Browsers automatically perform *hit detection*—the process of finding out which element the mouse pointer is over—for you; you simply need to register mouse event handlers for your DOM elements and controls. However, WebGL is only a drawing system and, as such, has no built-in support for hit detection. You need to build that yourself. Thankfully, Three.js gives us the support we need so that we can tell when the mouse is over an object. We will lean on that to implement rollovers, clicks, and dragging, as well as camera navigation. We will also use Tween.js to combine interaction with animation for some nice UI effects. Let's get into it.

Hit Detection, Picking, and Projection

Hit detection is a special case of the more general 3D graphics concept of *picking*, the process of determining if two 3D objects intersect. 3D picking is commonly used for hit detection, but it is also the basis for physics, collision, terrain following, and more. In this section, we will explore using picking to implement hit detection.

Recall that ultimately, 3D rendering in WebGL is a 2D operation that paints pixels in a 2D region of the screen. The pixels are generated by a shader, which takes 2D and 3D inputs, including a projection matrix that converts numbers in 3D space to 2D space, "projecting" the 3D image onto the 2D viewport (a DOM element in your browser window). See Figure 5-1.

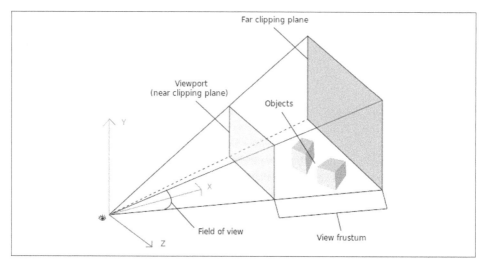

Figure 5-1. Camera, viewport, and projection, reproduced from http://obviam.net/ index.php/3d-programming-with-android-projections-perspective/ with permission

Hit detection of 3D objects in the scene reverses the process of projecting 3D images onto a 2D surface. First, a mouse coordinate is translated to viewport space (with the origin at the center and coordinates ranging from −.5 to +.5 in *x* and *y*). That viewport coordinate is then transformed into a 3D point that is the origin of a *ray*, a geometric entity with an origin, a direction, and an infinite distance. Our pick ray starts at where the 2D viewport coordinates intersect the near clipping plane, and goes straight back to the far clipping plane. Any objects that this ray intersects are considered "under" the mouse pointer.

Hit Detection in Three.js

Three.js provides us with classes to make implementing hit detection fairly easy. THREE.Projector does the matrix math to convert our 2D viewport coordinates. THREE.Ray has methods to find the intersection between the ray and objects in the scene such as meshes. We will be making heavy use of these classes to build our interactions.

I have wrapped up Three.js hit detection in helper methods within Sim.js so that you can quickly add mouse handlers to your objects. Let's walk through the mouse handling code in Sim.js before we move on to creating some examples. Example 5-1 shows the relevant code fragments from file *sim/sim.js*.

Example 5-1. Sim.js mouse handling and hit detection

```
// Event handling
Sim.App.prototype.initMouse = function()
{
    var dom = this.renderer.domElement;

    var that = this;
    dom.addEventListener( 'mousemove',
            function(e) { that.onDocumentMouseMove(e); }, false );
    dom.addEventListener( 'mousedown',
            function(e) { that.onDocumentMouseDown(e); }, false );
    dom.addEventListener( 'mouseup',
            function(e) { that.onDocumentMouseUp(e); }, false );

    $(dom).mousewheel(
            function(e, delta) {
                that.onDocumentMouseScroll(e, delta);
            }
        );

    this.overObject = null;
    this.clickedObject = null;
}

...

Sim.App.prototype.onDocumentMouseDown = function(event)
{
    event.preventDefault();

    var handled = false;

    var intersected = this.objectFromMouse(event.pageX, event.pageY);
    if (intersected.object)
    {
        if (intersected.object.handleMouseDown)
        {
            intersected.object.handleMouseDown(event.pageX,
                event.pageY, intersected.point, intersected.normal);
            this.clickedObject = intersected.object;
            handled = true;
        }
    }

    if (!handled && this.handleMouseDown)
    {
```

```
            this.handleMouseDown(event.pageX, event.pageY);
    }
}

...

Sim.App.prototype.objectFromMouse = function(pagex, pagey,
    calcDragOffset)
{
    // Translate page coords to element coords
    var offset = $(this.renderer.domElement).offset();
    var eltx = pagex - offset.left;
    var elty = pagey - offset.top;

    // Translate client coords into viewport x,y
    var vpx = ( eltx / this.container.offsetWidth ) * 2 - 1;
    var vpy = - ( elty / this.container.offsetHeight ) * 2 + 1;

    var vector = new THREE.Vector3( vpx, vpy, 0.5 );

    this.projector.unprojectVector( vector, this.camera );

    var ray = new THREE.Ray( this.camera.position,
        vector.subSelf( this.camera.position ).normalize() );

    var intersects = ray.intersectScene( this.scene );

    if ( intersects.length > 0 ) {

        var i = 0;
        while(!intersects[i].object.visible)
        {
            i++;
        }

        var intersected = intersects[i];
        var mat = new THREE.Matrix4().getInverse(
            intersected.object.matrixWorld);
        var point = mat.multiplyVector3(intersected.point);

        return (this.findObjectFromIntersected(
            intersected.object, intersected.point,
            intersected.face.normal));
    }
    else
    {
        return { object : null, point : null, normal : null };
    }
}

Sim.App.prototype.findObjectFromIntersected = function(object, point,
    normal)
```

```
{
    if (object.data)
    {
        return { object: object.data, point: point, normal: normal };
    }
    else if (object.parent)
    {
        return this.findObjectFromIntersected(object.parent, point,
            normal);
    }
    else
    {
        return { object : null, point : null, normal : null };
    }
}
```

Sim.App's constructor calls a helper, initMouse(), to add mouse down, up, and move event handlers to the DOM element associated with the Three.js renderer. Let's look at one of the event handlers, onDocumentMouseDown(). This method figures out which of our framework objects, if any, has been clicked on, and dispatches to its handleMouse Down() method, if it exists. To figure out which object is under the mouse at the time of the click, we have another helper method called objectFromMouse().

objectFromMouse() uses the Three.js projector and ray objects to do the dirty work for us. First, we translate the *x, y* mouse position passed into the event handler from page coordinates into coordinates relative to the DOM element. Then, we transform those element coordinates into viewport coordinates (a coordinate system with its origin at the viewport's center, and coordinates ranging from –.5 to +.5 in *x* and *y*). Now that our mouse data is in viewport coordinates, we can transform them into 3D world coordinates to be used to create a ray cast from the front clipping plane directly backward.

Once we have the ray, we call ray.intersectScene(this.scene) to find the objects that it intersects; those objects are the ones under the mouse pointer. This method returns a list sorted front-to-back, so we actually can find all of the objects under the mouse. For our purposes, the first one in the list is front-most, and therefore the one we want. We have to do one more thing before we can use the result: we call the helper method findObjectFromIntersected() to get the associated Sim.js object. It may be attached directly to the Three.js object, stored as object.data, or it may be attached to one of its Three.js ancestors. Once we have the object in hand, we can call its mouse event handler, in this case, handleMouseDown(). Sim.js also supports handlers for mouse up, mouse over, and mouse out in a similar fashion.

Implementing Rollovers and Clicks

Now that we have our hit detection code in place, it is very easy to add rollover and click behavior to a scene. Let's create a few simple examples to show how it works. For rollovers, we could use the old web programming trick of swapping images; this is trivial to do with Three.js, simply by changing the map property of an object's material. But with WebGL we can implement so many other, cooler effects, using color, lighting, scale, and animation, and as a bonus there is little need for artists to create additional textures for the rollover states.

Figure 5-2 shows a simple page with a set of user interface controls along the bottom bar. Each control is just a Three.js PlaneGeometry object with a PNG image that includes some transparency. Open the page *Chapter 5/interaction-simple.html* to run the example. As you move the mouse over a control, see how it highlights and gets bigger. Click on the control and it zooms to the front and center; click again and it goes back to its original position. This type of interaction is really easy to do with WebGL, on par with dynamic HTML effects, but it offers many more possibilities. Let's take a look at how it's done.

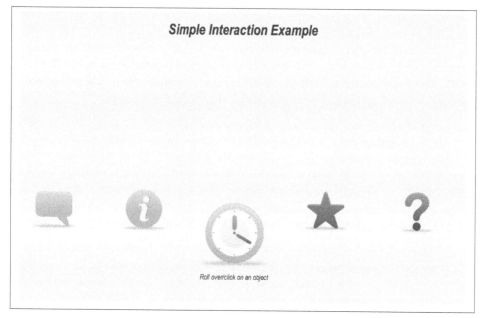

Figure 5-2. Rollover and click interaction; free icons from http://dryicons.com/free-icons/ preview/coquette-icons-set/

This example creates and lays out several instances of a Control object, which displays a rectangular graphic and implements rollover and click behaviors. Example 5-2 shows the code for the rollover effect.

Example 5-2. Implementing a rollover using scale and color
```
Control.prototype.handleMouseOver = function(x, y)
{
    this.mesh.scale.set(1.05, 1.05, 1.05);
    this.mesh.material.ambient.setRGB(.777,.777,.777);
}
```

```
Control.prototype.handleMouseOut = function(x, y)
{
    this.mesh.scale.set(1, 1, 1);
    this.mesh.material.ambient.setRGB(.667, .667, .667);
}
```

Easy peasy: when the mouse is over a control, we scale the mesh up a bit and we increase its ambient color. When the mouse is out, we set the mesh back to its original state. Taken together, the two property changes make for a nice effect. You may have also noticed that the mouse cursor changes to a pointer when it is over the object. This is done with standard CSS cursor manipulation. To make it easy, Sim.js supports an over Cursor property on every object. If that is set to a valid CSS cursor value, the hit detection code will automatically change the cursor to that shape when the mouse pointer is over the object.

To implement click behavior, we simply add a handleMouseDown() method. (We could also have done this on handleMouseUp()—it's really a developer preference.) In this case, we want to do something snazzy, so we are going to animate the control with a tween to zoom it to the front and center of the control bar. Example 5-3 shows the code.

Example 5-3. Implementing click behavior with a tween
```
Control.prototype.handleMouseDown = function(x, y, hitPoint)
{
    if (!this.selected)
    {
        this.select();
    }
    else
    {
        this.deselect();
    }
}

Control.prototype.select = function()
{
    if (!this.savedposition)
    {
        this.savedposition = this.mesh.position.clone();
    }

    new TWEEN.Tween(this.mesh.position)
    .to({
        x : 0,
        y : 0,
        z: 2
        }, 500).start();

    this.selected = true;
    this.publish("selected", this, true);
```

```
}

Control.prototype.deselect = function()
{
    new TWEEN.Tween(this.mesh.position)
    .to({ x: this.savedposition.x,
          y: this.savedposition.y,
          z: this.savedposition.z
        }, 500).start();

    this.selected = false;
    this.publish("selected", this, false);
}
```

Implementing Dragging

In 3D applications, you may want to allow the user to drag objects around in the scene.
That process is a little more involved than simple picking, because mouse-based dragging takes place on a 2D surface, while 3D objects exist in the 3D coordinate space. One
key to making this work is to constrain the dragging movement in some way, for example, to a 2D plane within the scene. That approach works well for moving an object's
position. Another possibility is to constrain dragging on the surface of a sphere, disk,
or cylinder, which is appropriate for rotating objects. Let's look at an example of dragging
on a plane.

File *Chapter 5/interaction-drag.html* shows dragging in action. Open it, and drag the ball
around on the screen. Also, try this: mouse down in the content area (not over the ball)
and drag. The whole scene will rotate. Now drag the ball again. It will still move in a
plane, though that plane is now no longer parallel with the screen. All movement of the
ball has been constrained to a 2D plane within its own local coordinate system.

Sim.js has dragging helper utilities, defined in file *sim/interaction.js*. Example 5-4 lists
some of the code from Sim.PlaneDragger, an object that constrains dragging within a
2D plane.

Example 5-4. The PlaneDragger class
```
Sim.PlaneDragger.prototype.init = function(object)
{
    // Connect us to the object to drag
    this.object = object;

    // We'll need a handle to the app for projection stuff
    this.app = object.getApp();

    // Create a projector object
    this.projector = new THREE.Projector();

    // And some helpers
```

```
        this.dragOffset = new THREE.Vector3;
        this.dragHitPoint = new THREE.Vector3;
        this.dragStartPoint = new THREE.Vector3;
        this.dragPlane = new THREE.Mesh( new THREE.PlaneGeometry( 2000,
            2000, 8, 8 ),
            new THREE.MeshBasicMaterial( { color: 0x000000 } ) );
}

Sim.PlaneDragger.prototype.beginDrag = function(x, y)
{
    var planeIntersects = this.getPlaneIntersection(x, y);

    if (planeIntersects.length)
    {
        this.dragOffset.copy(
            planeIntersects[ 0 ].point.subSelf(
                this.dragPlane.position ));
        this.dragStartPoint = this.object.object3D.position.clone();
    }
}

Sim.PlaneDragger.prototype.drag = function(x, y)
{
    var planeIntersects = this.getPlaneIntersection(x, y);

    if (planeIntersects.length)
    {
        this.dragHitPoint.copy(
            planeIntersects[ 0 ].point.subSelf(
            this.dragOffset ) );
        this.dragHitPoint.addSelf(this.dragStartPoint);
        this.publish("drag", this.dragHitPoint);
    }
}

Sim.PlaneDragger.prototype.endDrag = function(x, y)
{
    // Nothing to do, just here for completeness
}

Sim.PlaneDragger.prototype.getPlaneIntersection = function(x, y)
{
    var app = this.app;

    // Translate page coords to element coords
    var offset = $(app.renderer.domElement).offset();
    var eltx = x - offset.left;
    var elty = y - offset.top;

    // Translate client coords into viewport x,y
    var vpx = ( eltx / app.container.offsetWidth ) * 2 - 1;
    var vpy = - ( elty / app.container.offsetHeight ) * 2 + 1;
```

```
    var vector = new THREE.Vector3( vpx, vpy, 0.5 );

    this.projector.unprojectVector( vector, app.camera );

    var ray = new THREE.Ray( app.camera.position,
        vector.subSelf( camera.position ).normalize() );

    return ray.intersectObject( this.dragPlane );
}
```

Sim.PlaneDragger does a pick against a very large, invisible 2D plane geometry that spans the entire viewport. This pick is used to calculate 3D positions on the plane, and to calculate offsets from the initial position (at mouse down time) to subsequent ones (during mouse moves). Subscribers of the PlaneDragger translate their object positions using these offsets. PlaneDragger's initializer takes a Sim.js object as a parameter; we use that object to determine an initial position for dragging when beginDrag() is called. We also tuck away the Sim.App instance belonging to the object, because later on we will need its viewport information to perform the pick against the plane in getPlaneIntersection().

Now let's look at how Sim.PlaneDragger is used in the application. Example 5-5 shows the mouse handler code from *Chapter 5/interaction-drag.js*.

Example 5-5. Mouse handler code for dragging
```
Model.prototype.createDragger = function()
{
    this.dragger = new Sim.PlaneDragger();
    this.dragger.init(this);
    this.dragger.subscribe("drag", this, this.handleDrag)
}
...
Model.prototype.handleMouseDown = function(x, y, position, normal)
{
    this.lastx = x;
    this.lasty = y;

    this.dragger.beginDrag(x, y);
    this.lastDragPoint = new THREE.Vector3();
    this.dragDelta = new THREE.Vector3();
}

Model.prototype.handleMouseUp = function(x, y, position, normal)
{
    this.dragger.endDrag(x, y);

    if (this.animateDrag)
    {
        var newpos = this.dragDelta.clone();
```

```
        newpos.x *= Math.log(Math.abs(this.deltax * Math.E * 10));
        newpos.y *= Math.log(Math.abs(this.deltay * Math.E * 10));

        newpos.addSelf(this.object3D.position);

        new TWEEN.Tween(this.object3D.position)
        .to( {
            x : newpos.x, y : newpos.y, z : newpos.z
        }, 1000)
        .easing(TWEEN.Easing.Quadratic.EaseOut).start();
    }

    this.lastx = x;
    this.lasty = y;

    this.lastDragPoint = null;
    this.dragDelta = null;
}

Model.prototype.handleMouseMove = function(x, y)
{
    this.deltax = x - this.lastx;
    this.deltay = y - this.lasty;

    this.dragger.drag(x, y);
}

Model.prototype.handleDrag = function(dragPoint)
{
    this.object3D.position.copy(dragPoint);

    this.dragDelta.copy(dragPoint).subSelf(this.lastDragPoint);
    this.lastDragPoint.copy(dragPoint);
}
```

The code in boldface in Example 5-5 shows how we connect the PlaneDragger with the application. Helper method createDragger() initializes the dragger with our object, and adds a subscriber for drag events. On mouse down, we call this.dragger.begin Drag() to establish the initial drag point (in 2D coordinates) based on the mouse position. On mouse move, we call this.dragger.drag() to update the 2D drag position; the PlaneDragger in turn publishes the updated drag position in our object's local 3D coordinates. Finally, our subscriber method handleDrag() handles the drag event by moving the object.

You may have noticed a lot of other code in this example, not highlighted in bold. That code is in there to implement a post-drag animation effect, which we are going to talk about next.

Using Tweens with Dragging

Now that we know how to drag objects, it would be nice to make the dragging feel more natural. The gesturing interfaces pioneered by Apple in its touch-based devices have raised the bar on making electronic user interfaces feel more physical and intuitive. We can implement some of that natural interface style by adding tweens to our mouse handling.

Refer back to Example 5-5. There are several lines of code in there to save away current and previous values of both the 2D mouse position and 3D drag position. These are used at the end of the animation to create an easing tween. The property `dragDelta` is used to calculate a direction vector: after the mouse is released, our tween will animate moving the object in that same direction. Properties `deltax` and `deltay` are used as multipliers on the magnitude of that vector: the harder you drag in either x or y, the farther the object will travel after you release the mouse. Try it out by checking the checkbox labeled Animate with Ease Out.

Using Hit Point and Normal Information

You may have noticed a couple of other parameters in our example mouse down and mouse up handlers: `position` and `normal`. These values represent, respectively, the intersection point of the mouse with the object as a 3D position (known as the *hit point*), and the *face normal* at that intersection point. A face normal is a vector that is perpendicular to a polygon (face) of a mesh. Sim.js sends these parameters to the mouse handler because they can be quite useful. Let's say you want to know exactly where on a 3D object the mouse has been clicked so that you can display an effect or animation at that exact position. The `position` parameter tells you exactly where to place it; the `normal` parameter can help you orient it.

Have another look at the mouse event handling code in method `objectFromMouse()`, listed in Example 5-1 (files *Chapter 5/interaction-hitpoint.html* and *Chapter 5/interaction-hitpoint.js*). The Three.js method `ray.intersectScene()` detects not only which object is under the mouse, but also the position on the object that intersects the ray, and which face of the mesh was hit (from which we can extract the face normal).

Let's see what we can do with this information. Figure 5-3 shows a somewhat apocalyptic simulation of a spinning Earth with explosions. Trigger the explosion animations by clicking on the sphere. You will see flames billow out from the point at which you clicked, moving directly away from that spot out into space.

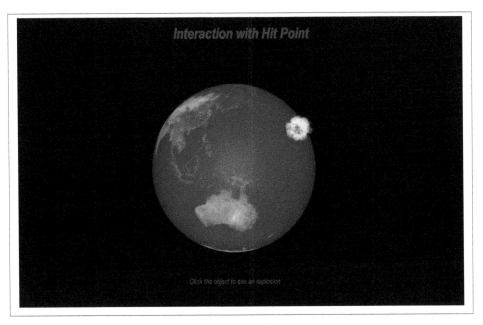

Figure 5-3. Interaction using the hit position and hit normal

Camera-Based Interaction

So far in this chapter we have shown how user interaction can make changes to content in the scene. That is fine for many types of interactions, but there will be cases when you won't want to do that. Let's say you are building a first-person shooter game, where the user can navigate freely within a complex environment. You could implement that with convoluted logic that moves the environment around, or you could take a more direct path: move the camera.

The Three.js camera (type `THREE.PerspectiveCamera`) is a first-class object: it can be transformed using translation and rotation, and its properties can be changed dynamically. We can combine this with keyframe animation to get some really great effects. For example, we can program camera "fly-throughs" that take the user through predefined paths within the scene at the touch of a button. (Now that you have learned the basics of keyframe animation and object interaction, you should be able to build one of those yourself!)

Some camera interactions are so common, and so stylized, that it makes sense to package them up into reusable utilities. Three.js has done just that with its *camera controls*; see the files in *src/extras/controls*. In this section, we are going to use them to implement common camera interactions.

The camera control utilities are a testament to the solid software design behind Three.js, as well as a great illustration of open source development at its best. Contributors other than Mr.doob largely wrote them, and they work beautifully with the Three.js core to deliver powerful functionality.

Implementing a Model Viewer with Camera Interaction

WebGL is a great technology for viewing models. Before WebGL, artists, engineers, and developers interested in 3D content would have to settle for a JPEG image preview, or at best some kind of animated fly-through. The only way to get a complete experience was to download a file and open it with an expensive authoring package, or obtain custom viewing software. Now, with WebGL, a model can be experienced interactively within a web page, without any hassle.

WebGL-based services are emerging that provide this capability for general use. The online service OurBricks (*http://www.ourbricks.com*) not only lets you view models in real time within its pages, but by simply copying and pasting a link, YouTube-style, you can also share it with others. OurBricks is a "prosumer" site, catering to indies, amateurs, and hobbyists; at the other end of the spectrum is the Autodesk 360 project (*https://360.autodesk.com/Landing/Index*), a WebGL-powered professional portal for designers and engineers.

But let's not allow these other developers to have all the fun. We can build our own model viewing application easily using the Three.js trackball camera control. Figure 5-4 shows a simple page with a really nice model, a vintage Camaro available for free from TurboSquid at *http://www.turbosquid.com/3d-models/blender-camaro/411348*. Open the file *Chapter 5/interaction-camera-model.html* and take it for a spin—literally. Drag the mouse around the content area of the window and you can rotate the model, turn it over, and look at it from all sides. Under the covers, the model is not moving at all; the camera is being moved in orbit around the scene's center, to the left and right (for pan) and in and out (for zoom).

Take a look at the source in *Chapter 5/interaction-camera-model.js*. We are going to skip over the code that loads the model, since we will be covering the content pipeline a few chapters from now. Instead, let's focus on the part of the ModelViewer application that creates camera controls. See Example 5-6.

Example 5-6. Using the Three.js trackball controls

```
ModelViewer.prototype.createCameraControls = function()
{
    var controls = new THREE.TrackballControls(
        this.camera, this.renderer.domElement );
    var radius = ModelViewer.CAMERA_RADIUS;
```

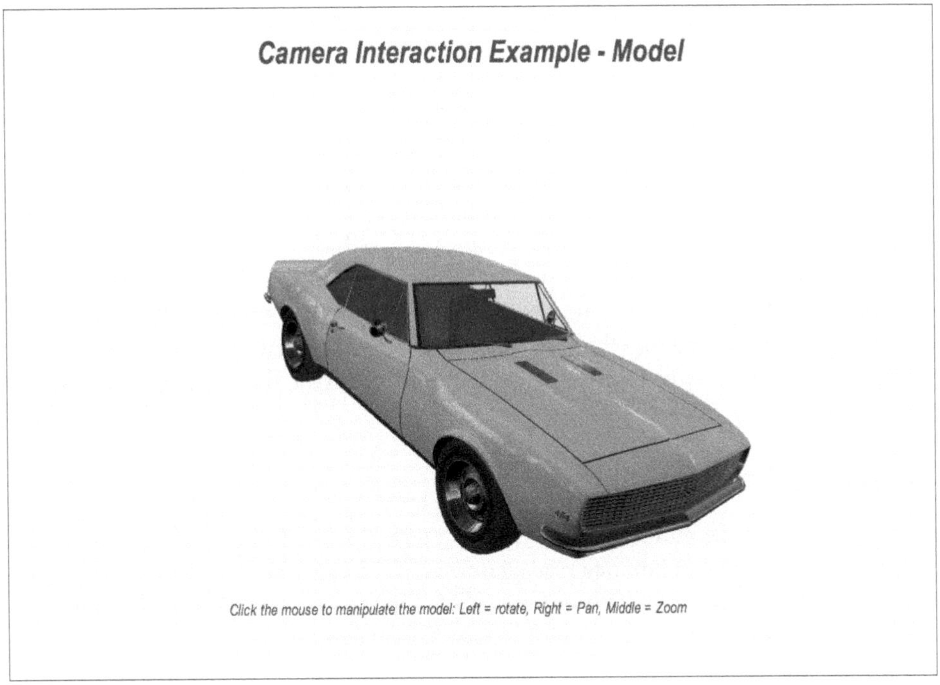

Camera Interaction Example - Model

Click the mouse to manipulate the model: Left = rotate, Right = Pan, Middle = Zoom

Figure 5-4. Camera-based model viewing with trackball controls; Camaro model by dskfnwn (http://www.turbosquid.com/FullPreview/Index.cfm/ID/411348)

```
    controls.rotateSpeed = ModelViewer.ROTATE_SPEED;
    controls.zoomSpeed = ModelViewer.ZOOM_SPEED;
    controls.panSpeed = ModelViewer.PAN_SPEED;
    controls.dynamicDampingFactor = ModelViewer.DAMPING_FACTOR;
    controls.noZoom = false;
    controls.noPan = false;
    controls.staticMoving = false;

    controls.minDistance = radius * ModelViewer.MIN_DISTANCE_FACTOR;
    controls.maxDistance = radius * ModelViewer.MAX_DISTANCE_FACTOR;

    this.controls = controls;
}

ModelViewer.prototype.update = function()
{
    this.controls.update();
    Sim.App.prototype.update.call(this);
}


ModelViewer.CAMERA_START_Z = 22;
ModelViewer.CAMERA_RADIUS = 20;
```

```
ModelViewer.MIN_DISTANCE_FACTOR = 1.1;
ModelViewer.MAX_DISTANCE_FACTOR = 20;
ModelViewer.ROTATE_SPEED = 1.0;
ModelViewer.ZOOM_SPEED = 3;
ModelViewer.PAN_SPEED = 0.2;
ModelViewer.DAMPING_FACTOR = 0.3;
```

The `createCameraControls()` method creates a new instance of THREE.Trackball
Controls, passing in our camera and renderer's DOM element. We then set several
properties on the controls, governing pan and zoom behavior, rotation speed, and min/
max zoom distances. With this in place, the `TrackballControls` object handles our
camera interaction automatically; mouse input moves the camera in various ways
around the object, based on which button is pressed. All we need to do is periodically
call upon `this.controls.update()`, which we do out of the application's own up
date() method. It's really that simple.

Navigating Within a Scene

One of the most common types of camera interaction is *first person*, similar to the
navigation experience in popular video games. In this style, the camera moves through
the scene to convey the sense of user movement. First person navigation has been pack-
aged up nicely for us in the class THREE.FirstPersonControls.

Launch the file *Chapter 5/interaction-camera-navigation.html*. We have a street scene
featuring that great Camaro model again, plus a few props (see Figure 5-5). You can use
the mouse and keyboard to move left, right, back, and forward, and to turn within the
scene. You can also move the camera vertically via keyboard keys.

Example 5-7 shows the code to add first person controls to the SceneViewer application.
We create a new instance of THREE.FirstPersonControls, passing the camera. We then
set a few properties to control how fast the camera moves and rotates. We also turn off
the ability to tilt the camera, which is sometimes useful but a bit too complicated for
this example; let's keep our feet on the ground. Finally, we make sure that our update()
method updates the camera controls too. Unlike the trackball camera, the Three.js first
person camera's update is based on time, so we need to pass in a time delta, which we
do using the Three.js Clock object.

Example 5-7. Using the Three.js first person controls
```
SceneViewer.prototype.createCameraControls = function()
{
    // Set up the FP controls
    var controls = new THREE.FirstPersonControls( this.camera );

    controls.movementSpeed = 13;
    controls.lookSpeed = 0.01;

    // Don't allow tilt up/down
```

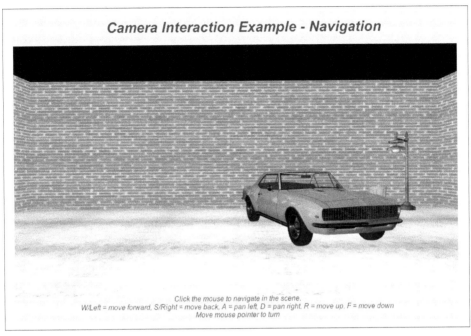

Figure 5-5. Camera-based navigation with first person controls; brick texture from http://wdc3d.com/wp-content/uploads/2010/05/red-brick-seamless-1000-x-1000.jpg; marble texture from http://www.public-domain-image.com/textures-and-patterns-public-domain-images-pictures/rock-stone-texture-public-domain-images-pictures/great-marble-texture.jpg.html

```
    controls.lookVertical = false;

    this.controls = controls;

    this.clock = new THREE.Clock();
}

SceneViewer.prototype.update = function()
{
    this.controls.update(this.clock.getDelta());
    Sim.App.prototype.update.call(this);
}
```

As you can see, Three.js makes it easy to incorporate camera interaction with a few lines of code. Personally, I would like to see a bit more flexibility in the camera control classes (e.g., with the mouse and keyboard bindings). But all in all, it's powerful stuff, and because it's open source, we can always get into the code and tailor it to our needs.

Chapter Summary

In this chapter, we explored how to make WebGL applications interactive. Using the built-in hit detection support in Three.js, we can roll over and click on individual objects as well as move things around on the screen. We can also combine mouse interaction with animated tweens to make our user interfaces more responsive and natural-feeling. For camera-based interaction, Three.js provides several handy controller classes that make development easy. This rich set of features combines with the raw graphic power of WebGL to enable a whole new kind of interactive web application.

CHAPTER 6

Integrating 2D and 3D

No doubt by now you have gotten a sense of the vast set of capabilities that comprises WebGL: the raw rendering power, the ease of development with JavaScript, the open specification, and the ubiquitous platform that requires no download. This is already a boon for all kinds of application development, a massive new weapon in the web developer arsenal. But it doesn't stop there.

Let's take another look at the official Khronos definition of WebGL (the italics are mine):

> WebGL is a royalty-free, cross-platform API that brings OpenGL ES 2.0 to the web as a 3D drawing context within HTML, exposed as low-level Document Object Model interfaces. It uses the OpenGL shading language, GLSL ES, *and can be cleanly combined with other web content that is layered on top or underneath the 3D content*. It is ideally suited for dynamic 3D web applications in the JavaScript programming language, and will be fully integrated in leading web browsers.

Obviously this is a mouthful, so we'll have to forgive the writers for trying to fit it all into a paragraph. But it's possible that the Khronos folks have—to borrow a term from journalism—buried the lead here. Look at the text in italics. In my opinion, the true breakthrough unleashed by WebGL—what really makes it different from any other technology that has come before—lies in its ability to be seamlessly integrated with all other content on the page.

3D graphics has been around for a long time. Even 3D graphics in a web browser has been around for a while, from early experiments with Virtual Reality Modeling Language (VRML), to the latest industrial-strength plug-in-based solutions such as Unity Player and Adobe Flash 3D. However, all of these technologies have traditionally suffered from being trapped within a fixed rectangle somewhere inside the page, with no hope of crossing that boundary. With WebGL, that restriction no longer exists. The pixels on the 3D canvas are combined with the other page content before the page is presented, in a process known as *compositing*. So you can treat the WebGL canvas like any other `<div>` tag on your page, layering it above or below other page elements into a unified presentation.

WebGL's integration capabilities go even further than compositing. We have already seen how simple it is to incorporate other content types such as images into texture maps; they're just URLs. But we can also create texture maps from live 2D `Canvas` elements and streaming video formats, allowing for incredible effects and new types of media experiences. Another equally important aspect to integrating WebGL is on the data side: because we write our WebGL applications in JavaScript and run them in a browser, we have access to every public API on the planet. This means we can create new forms of mashups and visualize data from a server in novel ways. Taken together, these features make WebGL not just another rendering technology, but a whole new *medium* with staggering possibilities.

Combining Dynamic HTML and WebGL

Say you are building a browser-based 3D game and want to pop up a screen on top of the canvas, maybe with a little transparency so that you can still see the canvas beneath. You'd like to do that in HTML; it's easy to write, it styles and formats the text for you, and it supports all the familiar HTML user interface controls. In the past, you wouldn't have been able to do it that way; you would have had to work with an alternate system that uses the 3D pipeline to present your 2D graphics. You probably would also have learned a new API and tool set; it wouldn't have half the features you had come to know and love in HTML, and it would have been hard—probably impossible—to fully match the styling of the outer page. Alternately, perhaps you want to embed an interactive 3D object somewhere within a web application and have the text and other graphics on the page appear with it, under it, or around it in a seamless visual presentation. That also wouldn't have been possible in the past—until WebGL.

The browser treats the WebGL canvas like any other element on your page. If you want to build 2D callouts that sit on top of your interactive WebGL-based interactive product manual, no problem: just pop up DIVs. If you want to embed an animated 3D object above the text on your page, you can: just put it in a WebGL canvas that uses a transparent background color and you will see through to the text beneath. In other words, integrating dynamic HTML with WebGL is as easy as using page elements. Let's look at a few examples that put it into practice.

Creating Pop Ups with DIV Elements

Dynamic HTML is the ideal technology for building pop-up screens and heads-up displays for WebGL-based games. WebGL does not have native support for drawing text (more on this later in the chapter); thankfully that does not present much of a problem here, because we can simply layer HTML above the WebGL content. We can also use CSS to style the user interface elements, thus perfectly matching the styling of the rest of our pages. Figure 6-1 shows the start screen of a make-believe space shooter game I just thought up, just now: *Shipster*.

Figure 6-1. Creating pop ups with DIV elements (planet texture maps and star background courtesy NASA/JPL-Caltech; spaceship models and textures by their respective authors; see the Examples README credits for details)

Launch the file *Chapter 6/integration-div.html* to run the example. When you roll the mouse over each ship, two things happen: the ship does a rotation animation, and a pop up, or *callout*, appears near the ship, presenting more information about it. The callout is rich with text information and a button control, but is otherwise mostly transparent, exactly in the style of a typical game heads-up display. Let's look at the code in the next few example listings, starting with Example 6-1.

Example 6-1. Code to pop up a DIV over WebGL (HTML)

```
<!DOCTYPE html>
<html>
<head>
<title>Creating Popups with DIV Elements</title>

    <link href="../css/webglbook.css" rel="stylesheet" />
    <link href="integration-div.css" rel="stylesheet" />
    <script src="../libs/Three.js"></script>
```

```
<script src="../libs/jquery-1.6.4.js"></script>
<script src="../libs/jquery.mousewheel.js"></script>
<script src="../libs/RequestAnimationFrame.js"></script>
<script src="../sim/sim.js"></script>
<script src="../sim/animation.js"></script>
<script src="integration-div.js"></script>
<script src="earth-shader.js"></script>
<script>

var renderer = null;
var scene = null;
var camera = null;
var mesh = null;
var theApp = null;

$(document).ready(
    function() {
        var container = document.getElementById("container");
        theApp = new Shipster();
        theApp.init({ container: container });
        theApp.run();
    }
);

function onSelectClicked(elt)
{
    var div = document.getElementById("callout");
    var shipID = div.shipID;
    theApp.shipSelected(shipID);
    div.style.display = "none";
}

</script>

</head>

<body>
    <h1>Shipster - Choose Your Ship</h1>
    <div id="container"></div>
    <div id="callout" class="callout" >
    <div id="header" class="header"></div>
    <div id="contents" class="contents"></div>
    <div id="selectButton" class="selectButton">
        <button onclick="onSelectClicked(this);">Select</button>
    </div>
    </div>

</body>
</html>
```

Example 6-1 shows the HTML for the game. The load handler function creates a new instance of the Shipster application, initializes it, and runs it.

The HTML file also contains JavaScript that handles when the pop up's Select button is clicked, by telling the app which ship was selected (`div.shipID`) and hiding the callout by setting its display style to `none`. Finally, there is markup in the body to define the container (our WebGL rendering window), and the callout that will pop up when the mouse is over the ship.

The CSS for this example is contained in file *Chapter 6/integration-div.css*. The CSS file is straightforward, but note that the `z-index` of the callout is set to 0 to make sure that it appears above the container element (whose `z-index` is set to –1 by default in the shared CSS file used by all our examples, *css/webglbook.css*).

Now let's look at the JavaScript in Example 6-2. For brevity, we will only include the salient code fragments. The full implementation can be found in file *Chapter 6/ integration-div.js*.

Example 6-2. Code to pop up a DIV over WebGL (JavaScript)

```
...

Shipster.prototype.handleMouseUp = function(x, y)
{
    var callout = document.getElementById("callout");
    callout.style.display = "none";
}

Shipster.prototype.handleMouseScroll = function(delta)
{
    var dx = delta;

    this.camera.position.z -= dx;
}

Shipster.prototype.onShipOver = function(id)
{
    var html = "";
    switch(id)
    {
        case Shipster.SHIP_FEISAR :
            headerHtml = "Fighter";
            contentsHtml =
    "Weight: 50,000 m tons<br>Max Speed:.6C<br>Guns: 4 fore<br>" +
    "Max Passengers: 4<br>" + "Freight Capacity: Minimal<br>" +
                    "Warp-Capable: No";
            break;

        case Shipster.SHIP_ENEMYSHIP :
            headerHtml = "Warship";
            contentsHtml =
    "Weight:66,000 m tons<br>Max Speed:.3C<br>Guns: 4 fore, 2 aft<br>"
        +
    "Max Passengers: 4<br>" + "Freight Capacity: Minimal<br>" +
```

```
                    "Warp-Capable: No";
            break;

        case Shipster.SHIP_CRUISER :
            headerHtml = "Cruiser";
            contentsHtml =
"Weight:100,000 m tons<br>Max Speed:.2C<br>Guns: 4 fore<br>" +
"Max Passengers: 8<br>" + "Freight Capacity: 5,000 m tons<br>" +
                    "Warp-Capable: Yes";
            break;
    }

    // Populate the callout
    var callout = document.getElementById("callout");
    var calloutHeader = document.getElementById("header");
    var calloutContents = document.getElementById("contents");
    calloutHeader.innerHTML = headerHtml;
    calloutContents.innerHTML = contentsHtml;
    callout.shipID = id;

    // Place the callout near the object and show it
    var screenpos = this.getObjectScreenPosition(this.ships[id]);
    callout.style.display = "block";
    callout.style.left = (screenpos.x - callout.offsetWidth / 2)+ "px";
    callout.style.top = (screenpos.y + Shipster.CALLOUT_Y_OFFSET) + "px";
}
```

First, the initializer for class `Shipster` (not shown here) sets up some lights and a camera, and creates and positions a planet in the background—the very same `Earth` from our graphics examples back in Chapter 3. Then it creates three `Ship` objects. The `Ship` class contains code to load a ship model, plus mouse handling and animation for the rollovers.

`Ship` publishes an over event, which is handled in `Shipster.onShipOver()`. This is where our callout DIV is populated with the correct information (by setting the `innerHTML` of the various elements in the callout) and then popped up by setting the callout's display style to `block`. We position the DIV using a helper method, `getOb jectScreenPosition()`, which we will cover in detail in the next section. `Shipster` also implements its own mouse handling so that when the mouse is clicked within the game window, but not over a ship, the callout is hidden again (see `Shipster.handleMouse Up()`). And that's pretty much the whole experience.

Using 2D Screen Positions to Annotate 3D Objects

In creating a heads-up display for a 3D application, you often want to position the 2D elements of the overlay with respect to the 3D objects being presented in the scene— either directly over them, or near them with an arrow or other callout graphic. We actually do just that in the Shipster game, with a little help from our old friend from Chapter 5, the Three.js `Projector`.

Example 6-3 shows the code for `Shipster.getObjectScreenPosition()`. This method is used to determine where the origin of a 3D object shows up in the 2D window once rendered. It takes as input a Sim.js object and the returns *x, y* screen position relative to the Three.js renderer's DOM element. Recall that `THREE.Projector` converts vectors from world space to screen space, and vice versa. For our interaction examples in Chapter 5, we did the inverse projection: we wanted to know what objects were under a given screen position. For our purposes here, we need to know the opposite: where a 3D object will actually show up on the screen.

Example 6-3. Annotating the 3D scene using 2D screen position

```
Shipster.prototype.getObjectScreenPosition = function(object)
{
    var mat = object.object3D.matrixWorld;
    var pos = new THREE.Vector3();
    pos = mat.multiplyVector3(pos);

    projected = pos.clone();
    this.projector.projectVector(projected, this.camera);

    var eltx = (1 + projected.x) * this.container.offsetWidth / 2 ;
    var elty = (1 - projected.y) * this.container.offsetHeight / 2;

    var offset = $(this.renderer.domElement).offset();
    eltx += offset.left;
    elty += offset.top;

    return { x : eltx, y : elty };
}
```

First, we obtain the object's position in *world space*. World space comprises not only the object's own transform information, but also all of the transforms of its ancestor objects in the hierarchy (if this is getting fuzzy for you, see Chapter 3 for a refresher on coordinate spaces and the transform hierarchy). The world space position is easy to obtain, thanks to Three.js: each object has a `matrixWorld` property that contains its current world space information, including that of its ancestor transforms. This method assumes that we are transforming the object's origin, so we multiply a new origin vector, `pos`, by the matrix to obtain the object's origin in world space. Once we have that, we use the projector and camera objects stored in our application to do the projection. Another vector, `projec ted`, stores the projected result in screen space. Finally, we convert those screen (window) coordinates to element-relative position with a little jQuery magic, and we can return our element-relative position. `Shipster` uses the returned position, offset by a bit in *y*, to place the callout just below whichever ship is rolled over and—*voilà!*—a true screen-relative callout.

Adding a Background Image to the 3D Scene

You may have noticed another bell and whistle in this example: the starry background. Unlike the solar system from Chapter 3, where we drew background stars using point rendering, this time we took a cheap and easy way: we used a background image. Take a look at *Chapter 6/integration-div.css* and you will see a line that sets the background image for the `container` DIV element (our rendering window).

```
background-image:url('../images/07.jpg');
```

The Shipster application contains a handler for the scroll wheel, courtesy of the jQuery scroll wheel plug-in by Brandon Aaron (*http://brandonaaron.net*). If you have a scroll wheel, or track pad that can emulate a scroll wheel, try it out: scroll forward to zoom in, back to zoom out. You should see the ships and planets move, but the stars stay still, as they would for a background of stars that are very far away.

So, what is going on here? Under the covers, WebGL is painting the background image before rendering the scene. Typically a WebGL scene has a *clear color*, an RGB (or RGBA) color used to paint the entire rendering window prior to rendering the objects. However, in this case, the clear color is done using the background image, and then any other objects are drawn on top of the image.

What a great cheat! We have created a compelling illusion of depth without any additional JavaScript code, and very little impact on the 3D renderer, just by using familiar old CSS and a bitmap. This is yet another example of how powerful WebGL can be in combination with other 2D graphics on the page.

Overlaying 3D Visuals on 2D Pages

The WebGL compositor works in both directions: not only can we layer 2D elements seamlessly atop 3D scenes; we can also place 3D objects on 2D pages and blend them visually with the page. The key is to create a WebGL rendering context with a transparent clear color so that the objects in the scene get rendered but not the background rectangle for the element. Let's look at an example.

Figure 6-2 depicts a web page with an overlaid 3D object. Open the file *Chapter 6/integration-object.html*. Look at that little alien guy walking around the page! Note the shadow cast by the figure, how it moves over the text on the page. Now, grab the alien with the mouse: you can drag him around. You can also use the scroll wheel to zoom the figure in and out, making it bigger and smaller. This level of integration between animated, interactive 3D content and the rest of the page opens up awesome possibilities. Imagine using this technique with online technical manuals, where figures, images, 3D models, and text blend together into a coherent presentation; or think about how it could be used to create new types of in-your-face interactive advertising. Let's have a quick look at the code.

Figure 6-2. Overlaying a live 3D object on a page (page background image courtesy ESA/ Hubble; UFO image public domain; alien model via Blend Swap; see the Examples RE- ADME credits for details)

The style information for this example is contained in *Chapter 6/integration-object.css*. The style for the `container` element, shown in Example 6-4, provides the tricks we need. Note the lines in bold. First, we define a background color for the container that is fully transparent, an RGBA pure white with an alpha value of 0. Second, we make sure the container appears above all the other elements, by overriding the `z-index` value defined in the shared stylesheet *css/webglbook.css*. And that's it: a 3D object moving around above the rest of the page!

Example 6-4. Stylesheet information for overlaying a 3D object

```
#container {
    background-color:rgba(255, 255, 255, 0);
    width:40%;
    height:40%;
    top:45%;
    left:45%;
    position:absolute;
    z-index:1;
}
```

There's an effect in here that bears mention: the shadow being cast by the alien. Three.js has built-in support for casting shadows. However, in this case we did not take advantage of it, because it only works if there is another object in the scene to receive the shadow, such as a floor or wall. In our example, we only want to see the alien and his shadow, to create the illusion of floating atop the page. So, we employed another cheap cinematic trick: we duplicated the mesh geometry of the alien, and then applied a simple gray material and a very compressed scale to flatten it into the shape of a shadow being cast on the ground. We then positioned and animated the duplicated mesh in lock step with the alien animation. Lo and behold: a perfect shadow. The code in Example 6-5 illustrates the hack in its full glory, implemented in the `handleLoaded()` method of the `MorphMo del` class.

Example 6-5. Faking a shadow with geometry, material, and scale

```
MorphModel.prototype.handleLoaded = function(data)
{
    // Add the mesh to our group
    if (data instanceof THREE.Geometry)
    {
        var geometry = data;

        // Set up a morphing mesh and material
        var material = geometry.materials[ 0 ];
        material.morphTargets = true;
        material.color.setHex( 0xffFFFF ); // brighten it up
        material.ambient.setHex( 0xFFFFFF );
        var faceMaterial = new THREE.MeshFaceMaterial();

        var mesh = new THREE.MorphAnimMesh( geometry, faceMaterial  );
        mesh.duration = 1000; // 1 second walk cycle
        mesh.updateMatrix();
        this.object3D.add( mesh );
        this.bodyMesh = mesh;

        // Fun! Fake shadow using a scaled version of the original mesh
        // plus shadowy material
        var material = new THREE.MeshBasicMaterial(
                { color: 0x444444, opacity: 0.8, morphTargets: true } );
        material.shading = THREE.FlatShading;
        var mesh2 = new THREE.MorphAnimMesh( geometry, material  );
        mesh2.scale.set(1, 0.001, 1.5);
        mesh2.duration = 1000;
        this.object3D.add( mesh2 );
        this.shadowMesh = mesh2;
    }
}
```

For this example, many thanks are due to Theo Armour, WebGL data visualization pioneer and technical artist/model wrangler who writes a blog at *http://www.jaanga.com*. Theo helped me find an awesome, animated Blender model and push it through the still-primitive pipeline to Three.js. Theo also thought up the shadow hack once we learned that Three.js wouldn't cast one onto a transparent object. Thanks, Theo!

Creating Dynamic Textures with a Canvas 2D

The designers of WebGL put a lot of thought into textures. As we have already seen, textures are created from web-standard image files using the JavaScript `Image` object. But you can also create them in other ways. The WebGL drawing context allows several different image inputs to the `textImage2D()` method, including `Image` objects, arrays of bytes, videos, and even 2D `Canvas` elements. Using a 2D `Canvas` as a texture means that you can create dynamic textures—also known as *procedural textures*—without resorting to writing a shader. It also means that you can program them in JavaScript using the popular and well-established 2D rendering context API that comes with the `Canvas` element.

The applications of procedural textures are virtually limitless. For our purposes here, we are going to have some fun by creating a little paint program. See Figure 6-3. Launch the file *Chapter 6/integration-canvas.html*. You will see what looks like a blank art canvas. Use the mouse to paint on it—literally. Click the mouse somewhere on the face of the canvas, and drag it around. As long as you are holding down the mouse button, circles of random size, color, and opacity will be laid down on the canvas, creating a one-of-a-kind, postmodern work of pure 2D flatness within a 3D space. Congratulations! You have just joined the Superflat art movement!

The term *Superflat* was coined by the contemporary Japanese fine artist Takashi Murakami, and lends its name to the postmodern art movement founded by the artist. It refers to flattened forms often found in Japanese graphic art, animation, and pop culture. More information and examples of the work can be found on Wikipedia at *http://en.wikipedia.org/wiki/Superflat*.

There are several things going on in this example: most notably, we are doing 2D drawing on the surface of a 3D object. But we are also driving the drawing from clicks within the 3D scene that get translated into 2D canvas drawing space. Let's dig into both of these pieces of code.

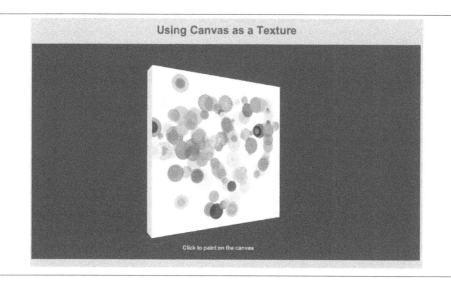

Figure 6-3. Using the 2D Canvas API to draw a dynamic texture

The file *Chapter 6/integration-canvas.js* contains the setup code for our app, but it's mostly the usual stuff. It creates a couple of objects: a 2D canvas view for drawing, and a cube behind it to create the illusion of a physical art canvas. The one interesting piece is the creation of the 2D canvas. Example 6-6 shows the code fragment that sets it up.

Example 6-6. Creating the Canvas element for use as a texture

```
// Create the Canvas and add it to our sim
var view = new CanvasView();
var canvas = document.createElement("canvas");
canvas.width = 1024;
canvas.height = 1024;

var param = {
        backgroundColor : 'rgb(255, 255, 255)',
        textColor : '#000066',
        } ;
var program = new PaintCanvasProgram();
program.init(param);

view.init({ canvas : canvas, program : program });
this.addObject(view);
```

CanvasView is a Sim.js object of my design. The initializer takes as input a 2D canvas element, and a *program* for drawing onto it. CanvasView doesn't create those itself, because I decided to leave that up to the application writer for maximum flexibility. In this way, the canvas element can be created either programmatically or from a tag in the HTML page. The program can be any object that implements an interface with a known set of methods for drawing on the canvas and handling mouse input. We will describe all this in a moment.

Beyond that setup code, there is nothing special in the main application file, so let's move on to the good stuff. *Chapter 6/canvasView.js* defines the `CanvasView` class. The code is listed in Example 6-7.

Example 6-7. The CanvasView class

```
// Custom CanvasView class
CanvasView = function()
{
    Sim.Object.call(this);
}

CanvasView.prototype = new Sim.Object();

CanvasView.prototype.init = function(param)
{
    param = param || {};

    var canvas = param.canvas || "";
    this.width = param.width || 4;
    this.height = param.height || 4;
    if (!canvas)
        return;

    var context = canvas.getContext("2d");

    var texture = new THREE.Texture(canvas);

    // Create our viewer object
    var group = new THREE.Object3D;
    var geometry = new THREE.PlaneGeometry(this.width, this.height, 16);
    var material = new THREE.MeshBasicMaterial(
            { map:texture, transparent:true, opacity:1 } );
    var mesh = new THREE.Mesh( geometry, material );
    group.add(mesh);

    // Tell the framework about our object
    this.setObject3D(group);

    // Tuck away needed objects
    this.canvas = canvas;
    this.context = context;
    this.texture = texture;

    // Connect the rendering program up to our view
    this.program = param.program;
    if (this.program)
```

```
    {
        this.program.setView(this);
    }

    this.overCursor = 'pointer';
}

CanvasView.prototype.update = function()
{
    // Run the rendering program
    if (this.program)
    {
        this.program.run();

        // Tell Three.js to re-render the texture
        if (this.texture)
        {
            this.texture.needsUpdate = true;
        }
    }

    Sim.Object.prototype.update.call(this);
}

CanvasView.prototype.handleMouseDown = function(x, y, hitPoint, hitNormal)
{
    // Marshall mouse clicks to the rendering program
    if (this.program && this.program.handleMouseDown)
    {
        var canvasCoord = this.calcCanvasCoord(hitPoint);
        this.program.handleMouseDown(canvasCoord.x, canvasCoord.y);
    }
}

CanvasView.prototype.handleMouseUp = function(x, y, hitPoint, hitNormal)
{
    // Marshall mouse clicks to the rendering program
    if (this.program && this.program.handleMouseUp)
    {
        var canvasCoord = this.calcCanvasCoord(hitPoint);
        this.program.handleMouseUp(canvasCoord.x, canvasCoord.y);
    }
}

CanvasView.prototype.handleMouseMove = function(x, y, hitPoint, hitNormal)
{
    // Marshall mouse motion to the rendering program
    if (this.program && this.program.handleMouseMove && hitPoint)
    {
        var canvasCoord = this.calcCanvasCoord(hitPoint);
        this.program.handleMouseMove(canvasCoord.x, canvasCoord.y);
    }
```

```
}

// Helper to convert object-space coordinates into canvas-space
CanvasView.prototype.calcCanvasCoord = function(point)
{
    // First, get corners of our rectangular canvas mesh
    var left = -this.width / 2;
    var bottom = -this.height / 2;

    // Now, convert those to UV space ([0..1] with +Y downward)
    var x = (point.x - left) / this.width;
    var y = 1 - ((point.y - bottom) / this.height);

    // Finally, convert UV to canvas coordinates
    x = Math.ceil(x * this.canvas.width);
    y = Math.ceil(y * this.canvas.height);

    return { x : x, y : y };
}
```

The initializer for CanvasView does several things, but the important stuff is highlighted in bold. We need to obtain a 2D drawing context from the passed-in canvas, and we need to tell WebGL that this canvas is going to be used as a texture (via Three.js, which just passes that information on to WebGL). We also, of course, need to draw the texture on a 3D object, so we create a mesh with that texture in the material, and a flat shape of type THREE.PlaneGeometry. The rest of the initializer is just wiring.

The next important thing of note happens during CanvasView.update(). This is where we actually draw the texture, by invoking the program's run() method. Note that we also need to tell Three.js that the texture is "dirty" (i.e., it needs to be re-sent to the WebGL graphics system because its contents have changed). We do that by setting the Three.js texture object's needsUpdate flag to true.

The rest of the code in this file is related to handling mouse input. Recall that the Sim.js framework contains code to dispatch mouse events to individual objects. Before we can dispatch the events, we want to translate them into a coordinate space the program can use for drawing. We do that in helper method calcCanvasCoord(). This method uses the information passed into our mouse handlers—specifically the hitPoint, or position in 3D object space—to calculate the mouse's coordinates relative to the 2D drawing canvas. We know that THREE.PlaneGeometry centers the plane about the origin, so first we offset the passed-in coordinates by half in each dimension to get our top-left corner. Then, we convert those into UV space ([0..1] ascending in x and y). Finally, we convert those coordinates to canvas-relative based on the width and height of our canvas element.

This particular implementation of calcCanvasCoord() works only for a flat plane with the default UV texture mapping of [0..1] in *x* and *y*; for other objects such as cylinders, spheres, or arbitrary meshes, we would need different algorithms to translate the coordinates. But this is about art, so let's keep the math simple!

Now that we have our CanvasView machinery set up, we can dive into the program that actually paints the pixels (see Example 6-8). *Chapter 6/paintCanvasProgram.js* contains the code for our class, PaintCanvasProgram.

Example 6-8. Two-dimensional rendering context drawing using the PaintCanvasProgram class

```
// PaintCanvasProgram - Simple paint program on a 2D canvas
PaintCanvasProgram = function()
{
}

PaintCanvasProgram.prototype = new Object;

PaintCanvasProgram.prototype.init = function(param)
{
    param = param || {};

    this.backgroundColor = param.backgroundColor || '#696969';
    this.textColor = param.textColor || '#aa0000';
    this.needsRedraw = true;
    this.running = true;
    this.items = [];
}

PaintCanvasProgram.prototype.setView = function(view)
{
    this.view = view;
    var texture = this.view.texture;
}

PaintCanvasProgram.prototype.run = function()
{
    if (this.running)
    {
        this.update();
        if (this.needsRedraw)
        {
            this.draw();
            this.needsRedraw = false;
        }
    }
}
```

```
PaintCanvasProgram.prototype.update = function()
{
    // If the mouse is held down, keep painting items under the
    most recent position
    if (this.mouseDown)
    {
        this.addItem(this.mouseX, this.mouseY, "rgba("
            +Math.floor(Math.random()*255) + ","
            +Math.floor(Math.random()*255) + ","
            +Math.floor(Math.random()*255) + ","
            +(Math.random() - .1) + ")",
            10 + Math.random() * 50);
    }
}

PaintCanvasProgram.prototype.start = function()
{
    this.running = true;
}

PaintCanvasProgram.prototype.stop = function()
{
    this.running = false;
}

PaintCanvasProgram.prototype.draw = function()
{
    // Set up drawing
    var context = this.view.context;
    var canvas = this.view.canvas;
    var texture = this.view.texture;

    context.clearRect(0, 0, canvas.width, canvas.height);
    context.fillStyle = this.backgroundColor;
    context.fillRect(0, 0, canvas.width, canvas.height);

    context.fillStyle = this.textColor;

    // Draw all our items
    this.drawItems(context);
}

// Adds a new blob to the canvas and flags redraw
PaintCanvasProgram.prototype.addItem = function(x, y, fill, radius)
{
    this.items.push({ x: x, y: y, fill: fill, radius:radius});
    this.needsRedraw = true;
}

// Draw each item in the list
PaintCanvasProgram.prototype.drawItems = function(context)
{
```

```
    len = this.items.length;
    for (i = 0; i < len; i++)
    {
        var item = this.items[i];
        context.fillStyle = item.fill;
        context.beginPath();
        context.arc(item.x,item.y,item.radius,0,Math.PI*2,true);
        context.closePath();
        context.fill();
    }
}


PaintCanvasProgram.prototype.handleMouseUp = function(x, y)
{
    // Stop painting items
    this.mouseDown = false;
}


PaintCanvasProgram.prototype.handleMouseDown = function(x, y)
{
    // Start painting items under the mouse position
    this.mouseDown = true;
    this.mouseX = x;
    this.mouseY = y;

    this.addItem(x, y, "rgba("
            +Math.floor(Math.random()*255) + ","
            +Math.floor(Math.random()*255) + ","
            +Math.floor(Math.random()*255) + ","
            +(Math.random() - .1) + ")",
            10 + Math.random() * 50);

}


PaintCanvasProgram.prototype.handleMouseMove = function(x, y)
{
    // Paint items under the mouse position
    if (this.mouseDown)
    {
        this.mouseX = x;
        this.mouseY = y;
        this.addItem(x, y, "rgba("
                +Math.floor(Math.random()*255) + ","
                +Math.floor(Math.random()*255) + ","
                +Math.floor(Math.random()*255) + ","
                +(Math.random() - .1) + ")",
                10 + Math.random() * 50);
    }
}
```

The init() and setView() methods are responsible for setup. The most important part here is that CanvasView calls setView() during initialization so that our program knows what canvas to draw into. Now for the good stuff: during its update cycle, CanvasView calls the program's run() method to do any drawing. PaintCanvasProgram.run() calls an update() method of its own, which will add new circles of random size, color, and opacity to paint on the canvas if the mouse is being held down. If anything new has been added, the needsRedraw flag gets set, which tells the program that it needs to draw to the canvas. We do this for performance, only invoking the full drawing code when needed; otherwise, all the repeated calls to the 2D API can degrade our frame rate. Obviously, if a texture is being animated or otherwise changes continually, you would not use this optimization. But this logic works well for our paint application.

Now, on to draw(). This is where we see the 2D rendering context API in action. First, we clear and then fill the entire canvas rectangle with our background color, using the 2D rendering context methods clearRect(), fillStyle(), and fillRect(). We then call a helper method to draw the items that have been added to the canvas. drawItems() loops through our item list, drawing circles of the specified size and color using the 2D context methods fillStyle(), beginPath(), arc(), closePath(), and fill().

The rest of the PaintCanvasProgram class deals with handling the mouse clicks, dispatched as described earlier in our walkthrough of CanvasView. If the mouse is clicked or dragged, we add new random circles to the canvas, which will get picked up for drawing next time through update().

And that's pretty much it: that's how you draw textures on a 3D object using a 2D API. Here we took a look at a single application of this feature, but I think you would agree that the possibilities are endless.

Using Video As a Texture

There is a lot of video content on the Internet. It sure would be nice if we could make use of it in our 3D applications. Maybe you want to build a sports game featuring a 3D stadium with a video Jumbotron display; or perhaps you are thinking along less prosaic lines, such as a video mixing system that presents and blends several video clips at once. Regardless of what you are contemplating, WebGL is here for you: it is trivial to create a texture from video. So let's do it.

Launch the file *Chapter 6/integration-video.html*, depicted in Figure 6-4. You will see six cubes, each displaying a video. Roll over a cube and it will spin; click on the cube to pause or restart the video. If you have speakers attached, you will hear a cacophony of audio as well. This barebones demo illustrates how to put video onto a texture. Let's dive into the code.

First, we have the HTML file, where we define the six video elements. The body portion of the HTML is excerpted in Example 6-9. Each video element is set to automatically play and loop; its style is also set to display:none so that it doesn't appear on the page.

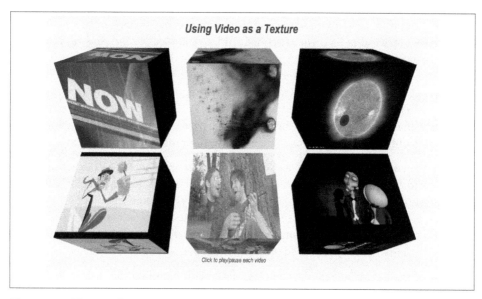

Figure 6-4. Using video as a texture; Pentagon news and moon videos public domainn; original short films courtesy of No Fat Clips! (http://dekku.nofatclips.com/)

Even though the video is set to not display, the browser will decode its pixels and associated sound streams. We are relying on this behavior to get the bits out of the video and blast them into textures in the 3D scene. Finally, we set the actual source of the video, the file that is to be played.

 The videos in this example are all in the Ogg format: an open media container format maintained by the Xiph.Org Foundation. Ogg enjoys some popularity amid the chaos of video formats on the Web today, because it is said to be unencumbered by patents (unlike MPEG and other formats). When using video in your web pages, take care to do some research into which browsers support which formats, and the associated IP restrictions. It's a bit of a swamp.

Example 6-9. HTML file with <video> tags

```
<body>
    <video id="video1" autoplay loop style="display:none">
        <source src="../videos/Pentagon_News_Sample.ogg"
        type='video/ogg; codecs="theora, vorbis"'>
    </video>
    <video id="video2" autoplay loop style="display:none">
        <source src="../videos/Specto.ogv"
```

```
        type='video/ogg; codecs="theora, vorbis"'>
    </video>
    <video id="video3" autoplay loop style="display:none">
        <source src="../videos/Moon_transit_of_sun_large.ogg"
         type='video/ogg; codecs="theora, vorbis"'>
    </video>
    <video id="video4" autoplay loop style="display:none">
        <source src="../videos/Anniversary.ogv"
         type='video/ogg; codecs="theora, vorbis"'>
    </video>
    <video id="video5" autoplay loop style="display:none">
        <source src="../videos/Floating Head.ogv"
         type='video/ogg; codecs="theora, vorbis"'>
    </video>
    <video id="video6" autoplay loop style="display:none">
        <source src="../videos/Motus et bouche cousue.ogv"
         type='video/ogg; codecs="theora, vorbis"'>
    </video>
    <center><h1>Using Video as a Texture</h1></center>
    <div id="container"></div>
    <div id="prompt">
    Click to play/pause each video
    </div>
    </div>
</body>
</html>
```

Now that we have videos in our page, we need to get them to display in the 3D scene. Let's look at the application creation code in *Chapter 6/integration-video.js*. This file defines a `VideoClass` app that creates six "video players"—simple cubes with video textures—and lays them out in the scene. Example 6-10 shows a few lines of code so that we can see how it's done. The `createPlayers()` helper method grabs each video element and passes it to the `VideoPlayer` class initializer.

Example 6-10. Creating the video player 3D objects

```
VideoApp.prototype.createPlayers = function()
{
    var sqrt2 = Math.sqrt(2);

    // Create the VideoPlayers and add to our sim
    var video1 = document.getElementById( 'video1' );
    var player = new VideoPlayer();
    player.init({ video : video1, animateRollover : true });
    this.addObject(player);
    player.setPosition(-2 * sqrt2, sqrt2, 0);
    player.object3D.rotation.x = Math.PI / 6;

    var video2 = document.getElementById( 'video2' );
    player = new VideoPlayer();
    player.init({ video : video2, animateRollover : true });
    this.addObject(player);
```

```
    player.setPosition(0, sqrt2, 0);
    player.object3D.rotation.x = Math.PI / 6;
...
}
```

Now let's have a look at the `VideoPlayer` class, defined in *Chapter 6/videoPlayer.js*. This class illustrates how simple it is to put video on a texture. In fact, the majority of the code in the file is there to handle the rollovers and animations, not the actual texture rendering. The code relevant to video texture rendering is excerpted in Example 6-11 and highlighted in bold.

Example 6-11. Initializing and updating the video texture
```
VideoPlayer.prototype.init = function(param)
{
    // Save away init params
    var video = param.video || "";
    if (!video)
        return;

    var size = param.size || 2;

    this.animateRollover = param.animateRollover;

    var texture = new THREE.Texture(video);
    texture.minFilter = THREE.LinearFilter;
    texture.magFilter = THREE.LinearFilter;

    // Create our VideoPlayer
    var group = new THREE.Object3D;
    var geometry = new THREE.CubeGeometry(size, size, size);
    var material = new THREE.MeshLambertMaterial(
            { map:texture } );
    var mesh = new THREE.Mesh( geometry, material );
    group.add(mesh);

    // Tell the framework about our object
    this.setObject3D(group);

    // Save away important objects
    this.video = video;
    this.texture = texture;

    // We'll start out with 'autoplay'
    this.playing = true;

    // Cursor rollover
    this.overCursor = 'pointer';

    // Set up the animation
    this.animator = new Sim.KeyFrameAnimator;
    this.animator.init({
```

```
        interps:
            [
            { keys:VideoPlayer.rotationKeys,
                values:VideoPlayer.rotationValues,
                target:this.object3D.rotation }
            ],
        loop: false,
        duration:VideoPlayer.animation_time
    });
    this.animator.subscribe("complete", this, this.onAnimationComplete);
    this.addChild(this.animator);
    this.animating = false;

}

VideoPlayer.prototype.update = function()
{
    if (this.playing)
    {
        // Don't update the texture until we have data
        if (this.video.readyState === this.video.HAVE_ENOUGH_DATA)
        {
            if (this.texture)
            {
                this.texture.needsUpdate = true;
            }
        }
    }

    Sim.Object.prototype.update.call(this);
}
```

First, VideoPlayer.init() creates a new THREE.Texture using the passed-in video element. It's basically that simple to set this up, except for one subtlety: by default, Three.js initializes textures with *mipmapping*, or *mipmap filtering*, a technique for antialiasing the pixels in a texture based on distance. It helps reduce creepy artifacts and "dancing" pixels as you move closer to or farther away from the texture. However, mipmapping is not supported for video textures, so we have to tell Three.js to use simple linear filtering instead.

Now that the texture is initialized with a video stream, the only remaining task is to render it. We do that in the VideoPlayer's update() method. We are going to assume that every time we are ready to rerender the video player mesh, we will need to rerender the texture because there is a new frame of video. (That may not be true in practice, but it's good enough for us here.) We add one more bit of sophistication, which is that we don't try to render the video at all until there is some frame data loaded for it. The HTML video element has a property, `readyState`, which tells us when this is true via the enumerated value `HAVE_ENOUGH_DATA`. Each time through `update()` we will poll that to make sure. If so, then we know it's time to rerender the texture, and we set the Three.js `needsUpdate` flag to make it happen.

Other than the few subtleties noted here, it is really as simple as it looks to add video textures to your WebGL application. Happy video programming!

Rendering Dynamically Generated 3D Text

No study of 2D/3D integration would be complete without covering issues related to text display. Over the years I have found that one of the biggest ironies with 3D systems is they almost universally lack built-in support for dynamically rendering text, flat 2D, extruded 3D, or otherwise. It's as if the designers assumed—and I can only conclude naïvely—that text rendering would never be required in a 3D presentation. Either that, or they inferred—I would argue wrongly so—that developers smart enough to get their brains around vertex buffers and matrix math would easily be able to master the intricacies of fonts, character sets, kerning, layout, and styling. Be that as it may, the fact is that most 3D systems don't provide text out of the box. WebGL is no exception. If you want to display dynamically generated text in your scene as a real 3D object, you have to roll your own.

Of course, with the full power of WebGL at our disposal, we *can* build our own text systems that use vertices to represent glyphs and paint them with custom shading. But I don't know many people who want to go down that road. It's a pile of work. Thankfully, there is a Three.js text extension that can help. It's very limited and far from perfect, but at least it gives us a starting point.

Figure 6-5 shows a simple application of 3D extruded text that is generated by an application. Pop open *Chapter 6/integration-text.html* and you will see extruded text, Superman logo-style, with a reflected version below. The text animates on its own, and you can also rotate it with the mouse. Let's have a quick look at how we built it.

The listing in Example 6-12 shows an excerpt from the TextApp application defined in *Chapter 6/integration-text.js*. `TextApp` creates three objects: two pieces of text and a plane for the "floor" on which the text is reflected. The reflection is just a cheap trick. We actually create a second version of the same text mesh and transform it to appear directly below the first text as a mirror image. The floor is simply a very shiny plane with enough transparency to show the mirror text below. This is all pretty straightforward. Example 6-12 shows a helper method for our `TextObject` class, `createTextMesh()`, which uses the Three.js text extension to create text geometry.

Figure 6-5. Three.js dynamically generated 3D text

Example 6-12. Creating dynamically generated 3D text
```
TextObject.prototype.createTextMesh = function()
{
    var textMesh, textGeo, faceMaterial, textMaterialFront, textMaterialSide;

    var text = this.str;
    var height = TextApp.TEXT_DEPTH; // depth means height here
    var size = TextApp.TEXT_SIZE;

    var font = "droid sans";
    var weight = "bold";
    var style = "normal";

    var faceMaterial = new THREE.MeshFaceMaterial();

    var textMaterialFront = new THREE.MeshPhongMaterial(
            { color: 0xffffff, shading: THREE.FlatShading } );

    var textGeometry = new THREE.TextGeometry( text,
            { size: size, height: height, font: font, weight: weight, style: style,

        material: 0,
        extrudeMaterial: 0
    });

    textGeometry.materials = [ textMaterialFront ];

    textGeometry.computeBoundingBox();
```

```
    textGeometry.computeVertexNormals();

    textMesh = new THREE.Mesh( textGeometry, faceMaterial );
    var centerOffset = -0.5 * ( textGeometry.boundingBox.x[ 1 ] -
            textGeometry.boundingBox.x[ 0 ] );
    textMesh.position.x = centerOffset;
    this.object3D.add(textMesh);
    this.mesh = textMesh;
}
```

THREE.TextGeometry's constructor requires several pieces of information: the text string to render; the size of the text (in world units); the depth to which to extrude the text (inexplicably named height); the font, weight, and style that define the glyph set for the characters; and the materials used to shade the front and sides of the mesh (named material and extrudeMaterial, respectively). Additionally, there are optional parameters for beveling and putting the text on a path, but we won't use those here.

As you can see, it is quite simple to add dynamically generated 3D text to your WebGL application. I will disclaim this, however, by saying that my experience with the Three.js text extra has been mixed. It may not support all the features you are looking for. But as a quick-and-dirty solution, and as a starting point for more elaborate text rendering, it succeeds.

 The text generation engine in Three.js was created by developer Zz85, who writes a blog at *http://www.lab4games.net/zz85/blog/*. It relies on web font support implemented in the typeface.js project (*http:// typeface.neocracy.org/*), an open source project to provide cross-browser font support. The font used in this example is the Apache-licensed Droid font (see *http://en.wikipedia.org/wiki/Droid_%28font %29*).

WebGL for Ultimate Mashups

Before concluding our visit to 2D/3D land, I want to touch briefly on a final topic: integrating data. Because WebGL applications are built with JavaScript, they have full access to the APIs that power the Web.

This means that developers can build new interfaces to existing databases, or mash up APIs in novel ways. I built a simple prototype of one such possible application: a "newsroom of the future" that brings together HTML, videos, and an RSS feed from CNN.com into a 3D presentation. Figure 6-6 shows the result.

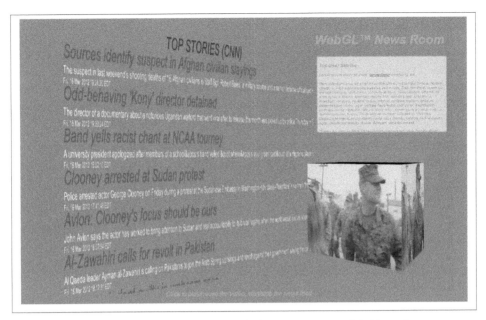

Figure 6-6. Media mashup with video, RSS feed on a canvas, and DIV overlays

The application can be launched by opening file *Chapter 6/integration-media.html*. The JavaScript in *Chapter 6/integration-media.js* does all the 3D scene setup, including creating a video player and an RSS viewer. The scrolling RSS display on the left is actually a Canvas-based texture map, created using the CanvasViewer class from our earlier example.

In this application, we utilize the class RSSCanvasProgram (see file *Chapter 6/rssCanvasProgram.js*) to display the RSS feed. To get around cross-domain restrictions with the feed data, the feed is actually going through a PHP script (file *Chapter 6/rssproxy.php*) running on the server, doing CURL calls to CNN, and returning the result as XML. The XML is then parsed by jQuery to give us back the items in the data feed. We display the results using the Canvas element's 2D rendering context API. It's not a fully formatted HTML display (since Canvas doesn't give us that easily), but we can at least style the title, description, and so on to create a nice display.

While this example is obviously contrived, it highlights the type of API mashups that are possible using the power of JavaScript, WebGL, and 2D/3D integration. Imagine that, instead of a newsroom, you could build an online social game using the Twitter API, or a giant "library of the world" frontend for public bookstore APIs, or a visualization of the global stock markets using public feeds (my friend and content wrangler Theo Armour has done just that; see his website, *http://www.jaanga.com*). These are but a few ideas. I'm sure you'll have many of your own.

Chapter Summary

This chapter took us through a huge grab bag of 2D/3D integration techniques. WebGL provides myriad possibilities for bringing together 3D content, page elements, canvas drawing, video, and text, and mashing them up with data and popular web APIs. With WebGL, the boundaries between page and scene, canvas element and rendered object, and video stream and rendered graphic all blur into a seamless media canvas.

With WebGL, the tyranny of the rectangle is officially over. Multimedia developers of the world, unite! You have nothing to lose…but window borders!

CHAPTER 7

WebGL in Production

Now that we have covered the basic capabilities of WebGL and explored hands-on coding, it's time to shift gears and talk about practical issues related to deployment. In this chapter, we will discuss a range of topics, including choice of engines and tools, file formats and delivery methods, and techniques for developing robust and secure applications.

Building applications in WebGL is a multidisciplinary exercise combining code and content, interface and database, art and engineering. WebGL applications have to be written with performance and robustness in mind, delivering a quality user experience throughout while gracefully handling adverse conditions. Further, given WebGL's current adoption—impressively strong, but by no means ubiquitous at this point—it must be said that developers need to be aware of which browsers and devices support the standard, and how to cope with those that don't.

The technologies underlying the WebGL ecosystem are the result of numerous global and local collaboration efforts—standards, open source projects, mashups, and even meetups—taking place against a rapidly changing web landscape. As professional web developers, it will serve us well to stay abreast of ongoing developments and be ready to adapt as the WebGL infrastructure evolves. Because many of the tools are new and evolving, consider this merely a point sample of what's out there as of this writing. Appendix A contains a list of online resources that will help you stay on top of these developments.

Choosing a Runtime Framework

As much as we have leaned on the fantastic rendering engine known as Three.js to quickly ramp up our WebGL learning, at the end of the day, this is a book about WebGL, not Three.js. I would be remiss in not reminding you that Three.js is just one of several 3D frameworks available for use with WebGL. Let's touch on a few of the noteworthy ones.

GLGE (http://www.glge.org/)
> A JavaScript library intended to ease the use and minimize the setup time of WebGL so that a developer can then spend her time creating richer content for the Web. I have worked with GLGE in the past and found it very easy to get around. In addition, it has excellent COLLADA file support (better than Three.js, in my experience).

SceneJS (http://www.scenejs.org/)
> An open source 3D engine for JavaScript that provides a JSON-based scene graph API on WebGL. SceneJS specializes in efficient rendering of large numbers of individually pickable and articulated objects as required by high-detail model-viewing applications in engineering and medicine.

CubicVR (http://www.cubicvr.org/)
> A high-performance object-oriented OpenGL 2.0 and OpenGL ES 3D engine, recently ported from C++ to JavaScript. It is used by Mozilla Labs as the basis for its WebGL projects and its Gladius game engine, a part of the Paladin open source game technology initiative (*https://wiki.mozilla.org/Paladin*).

The aforementioned frameworks are, like Three.js, focused on rendering, animation, and interaction. They are not game engines in the traditional sense of the word, nor do they deal with much in the way of application-specific behavior. However, each excels at something different and has trade-offs regarding ease of use, performance, and power. I chose Three.js for my projects because of its rich feature set and great performance. Three.js also enjoys a lot of popularity within the WebGL community and has a strong group of collaborators maintaining it.

The choice of framework is an alchemical mix of personal preference, business goals, and application requirements. Obviously there are no hard-and-fast rules here, but I will suggest a few things to think about:

Size
> Remember that we are delivering applications on the Web. The library needs to be small, ideally compiled and optimized with a build tool like Google Closure (*https:// developers.google.com/closure/*).

Strength

Different frameworks have different capabilities; make sure you find one that fits. Maybe in your case, out-of-the-box functionality is most important and you don't care about customization and extensibility. Or perhaps you need some really special type of rendering that one library specializes in.

Speed

There is no bigger turnoff (computer-wise, that is) than a 3D application with bad frame rates. Unless you have a really specialized application focused on rendering high-quality stills from large data, you should be looking for libraries that have been built with performance in mind.

Source

It may go without saying—but that's never stopped me before. Make sure that the libraries you choose are open source and that you fully understand the licensing terms. The ones I cited earlier are all licensed under generous open source terms, MIT and the like.

Support

I would be on the lookout for a framework that has strong community support, several key contributors, and ideally some industry or institutional backing. You want to have confidence that this library is going to be around for a while, that bugs get fixed, and that new features are being added to keep up with the changes in WebGL and the browser platform.

I strongly encourage you to conduct your own assessment based on the needs of your particular application. Check out the websites for each of these frameworks, and have a look at the many demos online. There is a lot of great stuff out there. You may even find that you need to write your own 3D rendering framework—though I promise that is a huge amount of work, so please don't go into it lightly! A more complete list of game engines, rendering libraries, and application frameworks for WebGL can be found in the Appendix A.

Loading 3D Content

In previous chapters, we glossed over the details of how content gets into a WebGL application. Now it's time to tackle the topic head-on. In this section, we will try a few different ways to load 3D content for use with Three.js.

It may surprise you that WebGL has no standard format for loading 3D content. Most other web media technologies come with an associated file format: think HTML, image formats such as JPEG, and media container formats like MP4 and Ogg Vorbis. Perhaps the only other exception aside from WebGL is the 2D drawing context that comes with Canvas. Maybe this design decision is indicative of a trend away from standardizing formats, and the inevitable slowdown in innovation that comes with that activity; perhaps it is simply part of the overall WebGL mission to Keep It Simple, Stupid, to make browser implementation more tractable. Regardless, I personally find it surprising and a bit troubling. I believe that WebGL adoption would move even faster when the industry standardizes on a file format to go along with it. I suppose time will tell. In the meantime…flame off!

Recall that WebGL is an API, not a runtime framework. It's also not a file format: the specification says nothing about how content is stored on disk, or how it is delivered to the browser; or even how it is represented in memory in the browser, other than defining the buffer structures that hold vertex inputs for the shaders. The job of representing 3D content—meshes (with associated vertices, normals, colors, texture coordinates, and such), materials, lights, cameras, and the transform hierarchy—falls to the application and/or the runtime libraries it uses.

Three.js has built-in support for a few feature-rich file formats. Unfortunately, with the exception of COLLADA (see the next section), all of them are specific to Three.js. There is a JSON-based format to describe single objects, and another one to describe scenes composed of multiple objects. There is also a binary equivalent to the JSON format, making for smaller file sizes. Finally, Three.js includes some experimental support for a compressed mesh format, further reducing file sizes. Let's look at how to load each of these. The code for the file loaders can be found in the Three.js source tree *src/extras/ loaders/*.

COLLADA: The Digital Asset Exchange Format

COLLADA is a standard developed and maintained by the Khronos Group, the same body in charge of WebGL. It is an XML-based file format originally developed around 2007 by Remi Arnaud and Mark Barnes, then with Sony Corporation. It has gone through several revisions over the years. From the Khronos COLLADA home page (*http://www.khronos.org/collada/*):

> COLLADA™ defines an XML-based schema to make it easy to transport 3D assets between applications—enabling diverse 3D authoring and content processing tools to be combined into a production pipeline. The intermediate language provides comprehensive encoding of visual scenes including: geometry, shaders and effects, physics, animation, kinematics, and even multiple version representations of the same asset.

For a while, COLLADA was very strongly supported in major digital content creation (DCC) tools such as Maya, 3ds Max, Poser, and SketchUp. Over the past couple of years, support and interest have waned, and there have been problems with compatibility and conformance among the various exporter utilities. However, it appears to be showing signs of renewed life. The OpenCOLLADA project (*http://opencollada.org/*) is dedicated to developing high-quality exporter software, currently for 3ds Max and Maya.

Let's look at some COLLADA content in Three.js. Launch the file *Chapter 7/production-loader-model.html* to run a simple model viewer that I wrote. I used a hardcoded list of sample files, to avoid having to write server-side code in PHP, Python, Ruby, or Node.js to generate a file listing. (That is left as an exercise for you, dear reader.) The interface uses the Three.js trackball camera controls first introduced in Chapter 5. Select the option Hellhound/COLLADA (.DAE) and you will see a scary-looking model of a monster dog. He should be walking in place, because there is animation data in this file. See Figure 7-1.

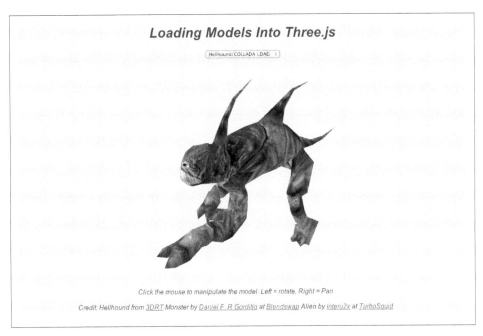

Figure 7-1. COLLADA model loaded with the model previewer; model via http://www. 3drt.com/downloads.htm

Before we get into the code for loading the model, let's inspect the COLLADA file itself. Open the file *models/collada_monster/monster.dae*[1] in a text editor. COLLADA is an

---

1. DAE, the COLLADA file extension, stands for Digital Asset Exchange.

XML format, with tags for describing vertex, texture coordinate, normal, and other geometric information, as well as the transform hierarchy, scene structure, cameras, materials and lights, and animation data. Poke around the file to get a sense of how the scene is put together. The following code snippet is a small excerpt. The file begins with the usual XML header, followed by the COLLADA document type tag and scheme reference. Next, we see an `<asset>` tag containing metadata. After that comes a whole lot of 3D data. If you are curious about the details of the COLLADA format, refer to the specification and other information on the Khronos website.

```xml
<?xml version="1.0" encoding="utf-8"?>
<COLLADA xmlns="http://www.collada.org/2005/11/COLLADASchema"
    version="1.4.1">
  <asset>
    <contributor>
      <author>Tim</author>
      <authoring_tool>3dsMax 8 - Feeling ColladaMax v3.04E.
      </authoring_tool>
      <comments>ColladaMax Export Options:
        ExportNormals=1;ExportEPolyAsTriangles=1;ExportXRefs=1;
        ExportSelected=0;ExportTangents=0;ExportAnimations=1;
        SampleAnim=1;ExportAnimClip=1;BakeMatrices=1;
        ExportRelativePaths=1;AnimStart=0;AnimEnd=3.33333;
      </comments>
    </contributor>
    <created>2007-12-05T22:27:58Z</created>
    <modified>2007-12-05T22:28:00Z</modified>
    <unit meter="0.0254" name="inch"/>
    <up_axis>Z_UP</up_axis>
  </asset>
```

Now, on to the code to load the dog. Our class `ColladaModel` handles the job. See file *Chapter 7/colladaModel.js* and the partial listing in Example 7-1. We use the Three.js class `THREE.ColladaLoader` to load our model, passing in a callback function to be called when loading is complete. That callback invokes `ColladaModel.handleLoaded()` to add the model to the scene. The data passed to the callback by Three.js is a full object hierarchy representing the content defined in the COLLADA file. We drop that into our scene and we're ready—almost—to show it off.

Because COLLADA models can contain animation data, we make sure we tuck that data away into our object in the property `skin`. Recall our discussion of skinned animation from Chapter 4: a *skeleton* containing a hierarchy of *bones* is animated using keyframes. Those bones plus additional data define how the vertices of the mesh are changed (*deformed*) with each frame. We process that animation data in our object's `update()` method, using some Three.js magic triggered by changing the skin's `morphTar getInfluences` property.

The use of morph targets (discussed in Chapter 4) in this example is not an accident or typo: the Three.js COLLADA loader actually translates skin data to morph target data internally. I imagine this was for simplicity of implementation, but it's not a great solution because it requires more memory and bandwidth (due to larger JSON file sizes). I hope the Three.js team eventually develops a more comprehensive and robust way to deal with skinned animation. But it works for our purposes here.

Example 7-1. Loading a COLLADA model with Three.js

```
ColladaModel.prototype.init = function(param)
{
    var group = new THREE.Object3D;

    var that = this;

    var url = param.url || "";
    if (!url)
        return;

    var scale = param.scale || 1;

    this.scale = new THREE.Vector3(scale, scale, scale);
    var loader = new THREE.ColladaLoader();
    loader.load( url, function( data ) {
        that.handleLoaded(data) } );

    // Tell the framework about our object
    this.setObject3D(group);

    // Init animation state
    this.skin = null;
    this.frame = 0;
    this.animating = false;
    this.frameRate = ColladaModel.default_frame_rate;
    this.animate(true);
}


ColladaModel.prototype.handleLoaded = function(data)
{
    if (data)
    {
        var model = data.scene;
        // This model in cm, we're working in meters, scale down
        model.scale.copy(this.scale);
```

```
            this.object3D.add(model);

            // Any skinning data? Save it away
            this.skin = data.skins[0];
        }
    }

ColladaModel.prototype.animate  = function(animating)
{
    if (this.animating == animating)
    {
        return;
    }

    this.animating = animating;
    if (this.animating)
    {
        this.frame = 0;
        this.startTime = Date.now();
    }
}

ColladaModel.prototype.update = function()
{
    Sim.Object.prototype.update.call(this);

    if (!this.animating)
        return;

    if ( this.skin )
    {
        var now = Date.now();
        var deltat = (now - this.startTime) / 1000;
        var fract = deltat - Math.floor(deltat);
        this.frame = fract * this.frameRate;

        for ( var i = 0;
            i < this.skin.morphTargetInfluences.length; i++ )
        {
            this.skin.morphTargetInfluences[ i ] = 0;
        }

        this.skin.morphTargetInfluences[ Math.floor( this.frame ) ] = 1;
    }
}

ColladaModel.default_frame_rate = 30;
```

And that's how we load COLLADA models. As I touched on briefly earlier, the format
has had some growing pains. Also, the support in Three.js is not great yet. These are
downsides to going with COLLADA, at least in a Three.js-based application. One big

upside is that COLLADA is a standard, warts and all, and many tools and frameworks support it. So at least it gives you, the developer, some hope that if you invest time and energy into producing content and getting it through a COLLADA pipeline, you can get the most out of it across applications, engines, and tools.

The Three.js JSON Model Format

In addition to COLLADA, Three.js can load scenes stored in a JSON format. The format was developed for Three.js, but in theory it could be used in other frameworks as well. You can have a look at a JSON model by running the model viewer and selecting the option "Monster/Three.js JSON (.js)". Keeping with our scary theme, Figure 7-2 has another monster for you.

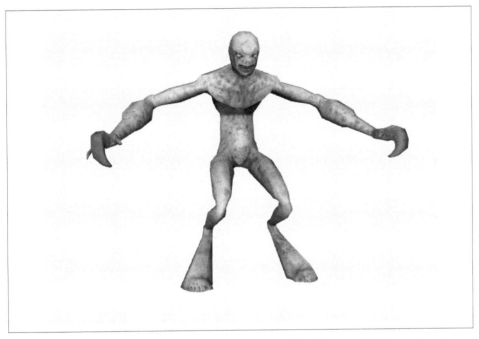

Figure 7-2. A model in Three.js JSON format; exported by Blender, CC licensed, authored by Daniel F. R. Gordillo, via Blend Swap (http://www.blendswap.com/blends/characters/monster-galera-man/)

The model for this monster was created in the popular modeling package, Blender, and then exported to JSON using a Three.js exporter utility for Blender. We will talk in detail about this exporter later in the chapter. The JSON for this model resides in the file *models/Monster/monster.js*. Here is an excerpt. After some metadata that includes information about the model itself and the exporter and version that created it, we encounter a list of materials (one item in this example), followed by some big buckets of data to represent the 3D information. Comparing this to the COLLADA example earlier, it becomes obvious why JSON is preferable in some ways: it's more concise, and loading is faster because browsers can load it directly into JavaScript data structures for us, ready to go. These factors may not have been the entire motivation for the Three.js developers to create this format, but they probably played a part.

```json
{

    "metadata" :
    {
        "formatVersion" : 3,
        "sourceFile"    : "monster.obj",
        "generatedBy"   : "OBJConverter",
        "vertices"      : 1020,
        "faces"         : 1018,
        "normals"       : 1017,
        "colors"        : 0,
        "uvs"           : 1271,
        "materials"     : 1
    },

    "scale" : 1.000000,

    "materials": [    {
    "DbgColor" : 15658734,
    "DbgIndex" : 0,
    "DbgName" : "Material_difz",
    "colorAmbient" : [0.0, 0.0, 0.0],
    "colorDiffuse" : [1.0, 1.0, 1.0],
    "colorSpecular" : [0.0, 0.0, 0.0],
    "illumination" : 1,
    "mapDiffuse" : "./textures/difz.jpg",
    "mapSpecular" : "./textures/spec.jpg",
    "opticalDensity" : 1.0,
    "specularCoef" : 96.078431,
    "transparency" : 1.0
    }],

    "vertices":
    [LOTS OF DATA]

    "morphTargets": [],

    "morphColors": [],

    "normals":

    "colors": [],

    "uvs":
```

```
[LOTS OF DATA]

"faces":
[LOTS OF DATA]
```

Our code to load the JSON model is similar to the COLLADA loading code. See the listing in Example 7-2 (file *Chapter 7/JSONModel.js*). We use the built-in `THREE.JSON Loader` class to do the hard work, registering a callback. There are a couple of big differences between this and handling COLLADA data: first, this flavor of the JSON format defines a single model, not a whole scene. (There is also a JSON scene format that can handle multiple models in a hierarchy. We are going to cover that later in the chapter.)

The second difference between handling JSON and COLLADA data in Three.js is in how materials are treated. The JSON format accommodates more than one material for a single mesh: some parts of a mesh can have one color, shading, and texture, while other parts can have other materials. Three.js defines a composite material type, `THREE.Mesh FaceMaterial`, for handling this. Our callback makes one of these materials, which signals to Three.js that the geometry object itself contains a list of the "real" materials to be used. Open this example in your favorite debugger, set a breakpoint in the callback, and have a look at `geometry.materials` and you'll see what I mean.

There is one more little detail to note in Example 7-2: in case normals weren't supplied by the author of the original Blender content, we call the geometry object's `compute VertexNormals()` method to generate them for us. Note that this is not a JSON-format-specific technique; it's just included to make sure the model looks smoothly shaded. We could have just as well included that call in the COLLADA callback from the previous example, but for that model it wasn't required.

Example 7-2. Loading a model in Three.js JSON format
```
JSONModel.prototype.init = function(param)
{
    var group = new THREE.Object3D;

    var that = this;

    var url = param.url || "";
    if (!url)
        return;

    var scale = param.scale || 1;

    this.scale = new THREE.Vector3(scale, scale, scale);
    var loader = new THREE.JSONLoader();
    loader.load( url, function( data ) {
        that.handleLoaded(data) } );

    // Tell the framework about our object
    this.setObject3D(group);
}
```

```
JSONModel.prototype.handleLoaded = function(data)
{
    if (data instanceof THREE.Geometry)
    {
        var geometry = data;

        // Just in case model doesn't have normals
        geometry.computeVertexNormals();

        var material = new THREE.MeshFaceMaterial();
        var mesh = new THREE.Mesh( geometry, material  );
        mesh.scale.copy(this.scale);
        this.object3D.add( mesh );
    }
}
```

Based on the number of JSON content files included with the Three.js sample code, this format seems to be the Three.js team's preferred way to get content into the runtime system. It has distinct advantages over the COLLADA format, as noted earlier. But I will caution that, while in theory this JSON format could be loaded into other frameworks, right now it is built for Three.js. It is hardly a standard, and it needs work. Still, all in all, it gets the job done.

The Three.js Binary Model Format

If you browse the *examples* folder or take a tour through the Three.js set of demos, you will notice that these text-based model files can get pretty big. It's wonderful for us engineers to have readable clear text for development and debugging, but it would also be nice to have a more compact format to work with. Thankfully, Three.js has a binary equivalent to its text-based JSON format. Run the model viewer again and choose the option "Alien/Three.js Binary (.js)," and you'll see our final monster. This one is in the Three.js binary format, converted from a Wavefront OBJ model I downloaded from TurboSquid. (We'll talk about the OBJ to Three.js converter shortly.) The result is depicted in Figure 7-3.

The converted binary model resides in two files: *models/alien2_obj/alien2_bin.bin*, which holds the bulk of the 3D data, and a wrapper file, *models/alien2_obj/ alien2_bin.js*, which contains metadata and materials. Here is the tiny wrapper file, in its entirety.

```
{

    "metadata" :
    {
        "formatVersion" : 3,
        "sourceFile"    : "alien2.obj",
        "generatedBy"   : "OBJConverter",
```

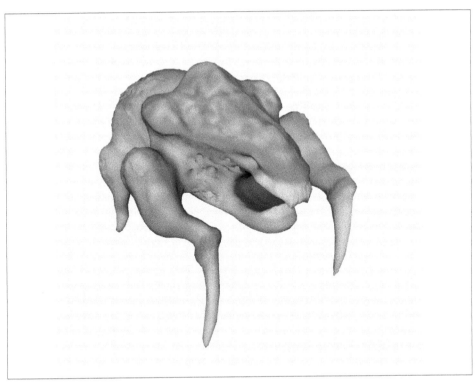

Figure 7-3. A model in Three.js binary format; authored by Interu2x, via TurboSquid (http://www.turbosquid.com/FullPreview/Index.cfm/ID/611477)

```
        "vertices"      : 4710,
        "faces"         : 9416,
        "normals"       : 0,
        "uvs"           : 37664,
        "materials"     : 1
    },

    "materials": [    {
    "DbgColor" : 15658734,
    "DbgIndex" : 0,
    "DbgName" : "mat1",
    "mapDiffuse" : "alien2Tex1.bmp"
    }],

    "buffers": "alien2_bin.bin"

}
```

We can't look at the binary file in any easy way, so instead let's have a look at the resultant gain: folder *models/alien2_obj* contains the equivalent model as a clear text JSON file. In text form, the file *alien2.js* is more than 1 MB; in binary, *alien2_bin.bin* is around 600 KB, a little more than half the size.

Loading the binary file is straightforward: just create an object of type `THREE.Binary Loader`. The file *Chapter 7/binaryModel.js* shows the source code for it. Other than invoking a different Three.js loader class, the code for handling this format is identical to the clear text JSON code.

3D Model Compression

While the Three.js binary format is more compact than clear text, we can do better. 3D developers are continually striving to make data more economical, and this need is particularly important for web delivery. The open source webgl-loader project (*http://code.google.com/p/webgl-loader/*) is one such initiative, and the UTF-8-encoded format that it defines for compressing geometry files looks promising. The Three.js examples contain a demo of loading it with the class `THREE.UTF8Loader`. Note that webgl-loader is not a standard, nor it is designed for Three.js. It's simply an interesting avenue of research and development that the Three.js team has been experimenting with.

The Three.js JSON Scene Format

It's all well and good to have an easy way to load single models into our WebGL applications. But in practice, it is far more likely that we will want to load multiple models, or an entire scene, at one go. Three.js also supports a JSON-based scene format. It defines scenes with transform hierarchy, libraries of materials and textures, lights, and cameras. In other words, it's a more complete format akin to COLLADA and earlier standards such as VRML and X3D. It can also reference individual JSON models residing in external JavaScript files, making for a modular pipeline.

For our sample, it's time to get away from the scary monsters and explore a softer theme. I found a gorgeous scene on Blend Swap (*http://www.blendswap.com/*), a great site for sharing Blender models. Figure 7-4 shows Kinoko, a cute cartoon bunny creature, perched atop a magic mushroom. To view it, open *Chapter 7/production-loader-scene.html*.

Browse through the JSON scene file in *models/Kinoko/character_kinoko.js* to get a sense of how the scene format is laid out. It's pretty straightforward, listing the objects and the transform hierarchy, and any materials, textures, cameras, and lights that will be used in the scene. Individual meshes reside in their own JSON files and are incorporated into the scene via URL reference.

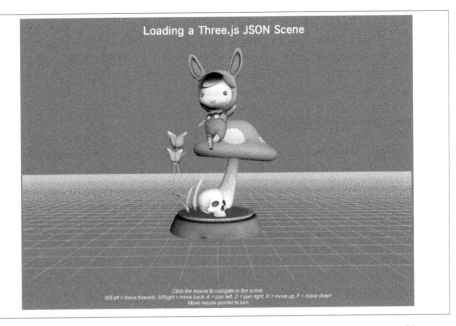

Figure 7-4. A scene defined in Three.js JSON scene format; CC licensed, authored by Kurama, via Blend Swap (http://www.blendswap.com/blends/characters/animecharacter/)

Loading a Three.js scene file into your application is easy: just invoke the `THREE.Sce neLoader` class. The callback handling is similar to the COLLADA handling: just add the returned result into your scene and you're ready to go. Have a look at *Chapter 7/ sceneData.js* for details.

Creating 3D Content

Thus far all the content we have seen in this chapter was created by artists. They may range in skill level and professional experience, but they are artists nonetheless. What I'm getting at is this: they're not programmers. I'm doing my best to avoid programmer-art in a graphics book, and, trust me, you especially don't want to see *my* programmer-art. You can thank me later.

3D artists use modeling tools. As with other web development, we need a way to connect their work into the overall flow of developing our WebGL applications (i.e., a content pipeline). The content pipeline for WebGL and Three.js is young and rapidly evolving. Thankfully, there is much active development, within the Three.js team of collaborators and in the community in general. In this section we will highlight a few tools and scenarios for creating and converting content to make it WebGL-ready.

This is a topic of paramount importance; eventually, the majority of content in WebGL applications will have been created by an artist's modeling or illustration tool, not a programmer's text editor. As of now, we are still at the "stone tools" stage of WebGL, with the pipeline being strung together for each project. That will change over time, but for now we will have to suffer through some discomfort with the tool set. We are the pioneers, blazing a trail to the brave new world.

Exporting Art from Blender

Blender (*http://www.blender.org/*) is a free, open source, cross-platform suite of tools for 3D creation. It runs on all major operating systems and is licensed under the GNU General Public License (GPL). Blender was created by Dutch software developer Ton Roosendaal, and is maintained by the Blender Foundation, a Netherlands-based non-profit organization. Blender is wildly popular, with the foundation estimating 2 million users. It is used by artists and engineers from hobbyist/student level to professional.

The monster in Figure 7-2 and the Kinoko scene depicted in Figure 7-4 were both converted to Three.js JSON by exporting models from Blender, using an exporter plug-in included with the Three.js distribution. Let's see how to do it. First, we need to get set up. Here are the steps:

1. Install Blender from the website. Make sure your Blender install works by launching the application.

   Install the Three.js exporter plug-in for Blender. You do that by copying the exporter plug-in from *utils/exporters/blender/2.60/scripts/addons/io_mesh_threejs* under the Three.js source tree (copy the whole folder) into the plug-ins folder of the Blender application package. The instructions for doing that vary from one operating system to the next. For example, my Blender was installed on my machine in */Applications/ blender-2.61-release-OSX_10.6_x86_64/blender.app/* and the plug-ins folder is under there in *Contents/MacOS/2.61/scripts/addons*.

   There is a helpful thread on how to do all this in the Three.js GitHub issues forum, *https://github.com/mrdoob/three.js/issues/143*.

2. Enable the plug-in. In Blender, go to File→Preferences, and click on the Addons tab. Somewhere on that long list to the right, you will see an option for "Import-Export: three.js format". Make sure that option is checked.

OK, hopefully you were able to get that working. If so, when you launch Blender, you can choose File→Export and you should see a menu item labeled "Three.js (js)". Open a Blender scene and run the exporter. The screenshot in Figure 7-5 shows the exporter in action. The exporter options come up in a side pane in Blender. My configuration (presumably the default) shows that on the lower left. See the highlighted rectangle.

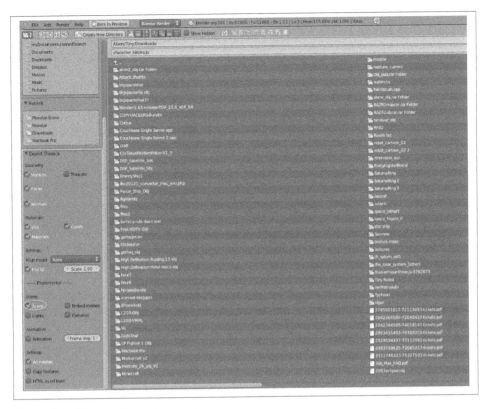

Figure 7-5. Blender Three.js exporter

The exporter has several options. I won't go into all the details here, but there are a few important ones:

Vertices, Faces, and Normals

These control the geometry output. If you're just getting started and aren't sure which should be checked, make sure they are all checked.

UVs, Materials, and Colors

These control material output. Without these checked you won't see your materials. But that may be what you want.

Scene

For exporting single objects, such as the monster from earlier in the chapter, make sure this is unchecked. For exporting scenes, make sure it is checked but there is a caveat: make sure that "Embed meshes" is unchecked; the scene exporting is still pretty experimental (as the label in the UI implies) and I was easily able to crash it within Blender with this flag turned on. If you export a scene, make sure you do it into its own folder, because each individual mesh is exported into its own JSON file that is referenced by the main exported file. Have a look at *models/Kinoko* in the examples to see how it is laid out.

Once you have this working, the fun begins. As is pretty typical with an export process, a few things can go wrong. The author of a file may have hardcoded texture paths in, and you'll wind up with references to files on Steve's F: drive, which you'll have to clean up. Or perhaps the textures were originally in BMP or Targa files. Everything will export fine, but Three.js won't be able to handle the textures. Or you may export fine but find a blocky, flat-shaded model when you view it, because you forgot to export the normals (and so on). Welcome to the Wild West, and happy exporting!

Converting OBJ Files to Three.js JSON Format

Sometimes it's easier to convert an existing model with a command-line tool. Three.js comes with a utility for converting the Wavefront Technologies OBJ format. The tool is written in Python. It's simple to use and only has a few options. To run the converter, make sure you have Python on your machine; I am running Python version 2.7.1.

This is the command I used to convert the alien bug in Figure 7-3 to plain text JSON:

```
python <path-to-three.js>/utils/exporters/convert_obj_three.py \
-i alien2.obj -o alien2.js
```

Converting OBJ Files to Three.js Binary Format

The Three.js OBJ converter allows you to generate a binary version instead of the clear text JSON, using the -t flag. This is the command I used to convert the alien bug to its binary version:

```
python <path-to-three.js>/utils/exporters/convert_obj_three.py \
-i alien2.obj -o alien2_bin.js -t binary
```

Converting from Other Tools and Formats

Blender is by no means the leading commercial modeling package. Nor is OBJ the top 3D format. But they are both popular, and free. That's why they are being used heavily with Three.js; the DNA just lines up nicely. There are many other great tools and formats, and it seems that we are seeing new support for WebGL daily. A fun thing I saw recently was a game demo created by AlteredQualia (*http://alteredqualia.com/*), one of the main

Three.js collaborators, that uses *Quake* models converted from the MD2 file format. See Figure 7-6 for a screenshot. The MD2 animated characters came from the popular site Planet Quake (*http://planetquake.gamespy.com/*). The converter can be found at *http://oos.moxiecode.com/blog/*.

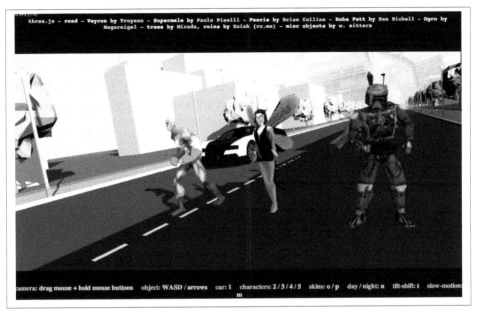

Figure 7-6. WebGL road demo by AlteredQualia, featuring MD2 models (http://alteredqualia.com/three/examples/webgl_road.html)

Browser Realities

Friends, we have made it through nearly seven chapters—practically the whole book—and up to now we've been able to avoid it, but we can't any longer. It's time to acknowledge the elephant in the room. It's a big critter, of a species native to the Northwestern United States and quite populous. Here it is: WebGL is not supported in all browsers, in particular, Microsoft Internet Explorer (IE).

Until fairly recently, this situation would have spelled death for WebGL. But times have changed. Depending on whom you talk to and what online surveys you read, IE is no longer the dominant browser it was back in the '00s. It now has less than 50% market share overall, and the installed base of browsers that support WebGL (Chrome, Firefox, Safari, and Opera) combined represents hundreds of millions of users. That's not as big as the adoption of Flash Player, but it is bigger than Unity Player, the leading 3D plug-in solution. So it's a healthy number, and bodes very well for the future health and well-being of WebGL.

Still, I don't want to sugarcoat the story. Clearly, not having IE on board represents an impediment for WebGL's adoption. There are some developers who won't touch the API if only for this reason. On the other hand, other developers are OK with requiring specific browsers for their application. And there is always the hope that Microsoft will someday get on board when it realizes the inevitability of WebGL. Maybe someday Microsoft will do it. Hope springs eternal.

Regarding other browser platforms, the Safari situation is a little gray. If you have a recent version, WebGL is in there. However, it is not turned on by default. You have to enable it using preferences only available in Developer mode, which is hardly ideal. But, hopefully, that will change in the future. As for mobile devices, WebGL is a bit early. Several Android devices have already shipped with WebGL, and the RIM Playbook comes with it preinstalled. As for iOS, WebGL is there in limited form only, as part of the iAd framework. All in all, we haven't reached WebGL nirvana just yet, but these developments augur favorably!

Detecting WebGL Support in Your Browser

Given the foregoing, it makes sense to code your WebGL application defensively in case a user's browser doesn't support the API. Let's look at how to do that. Note that there is nothing in this section specific to Three.js; this technique will work equally well with any framework.

To run this sample, you will need to use a browser that does not support WebGL, or disable WebGL in your browser. On my MacBook Air, I run this on Safari, which has WebGL turned off by default. Launch the file *Chapter 7/production-detect-webgl.html*. You should see a browser window that looks like Figure 7-7.

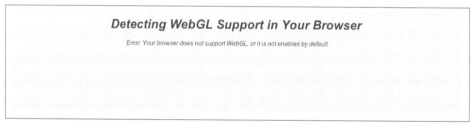

Figure 7-7. Browser detect result without WebGL enabled (Safari on Mac OS X)

The code to detect WebGL is in the file *sim/webGLDetector.js*. See the listing in Example 7-3. The class WebGLDetector contains a single method, detectWebGL(). This method will throw an exception if WebGL support is not present. The script code in the main HTML file catches that error and places the error message into the container DIV. The lines of code in bold contain the important logic: if the canvas throws an exception when asked for a drawing context of type `experimental-webgl`, we know there is no WebGL support.

Example 7-3. Code to detect WebGL support

```
// Simple WebGL Detector
Sim.WebGLDetector = {

    detectWebGL : function()
    {
        var canvas = document.createElement("canvas");

        var gl = null;
        var msg = "Your browser does not support WebGL, " +
            "or it is not enabled by default.";
        try
        {
            gl = canvas.getContext("experimental-webgl");
        }
        catch (e)
        {
            msg = "Error creating WebGL Context!: " + e.toString();
        }

        if (!gl)
        {
            throw new Error(msg);
        }
    },

};
```

Turning WebGL On in Safari

So, how do we know if the code in Example 7-3 works when WebGL *is* supported? Let's answer that by way of showing you how to turn WebGL on in Safari. Once it's turned on, we'll test the same example again. (Of course, we could always just run this same sample in a WebGL-enabled browser, but where's the fun in that?)

Safari has a Develop menu, which is turned off by default. Turn that on by selecting Safari→Preferences and selecting the Advanced tab. You should see a dialog that looks like Figure 7-8. Check the "Show Develop menu in menu bar" checkbox. Now we're almost there. One final step: go to the Develop menu (which should now be visible) and check the menu item Enable WebGL. You should be good to go.

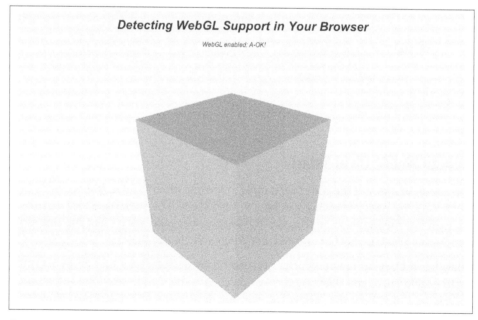

Figure 7-8. Enabling the Develop menu in Safari

Now run the example again by launching the file *Chapter 7/production-detect-webgl.html.* Your browser window should look like the screenshot in Figure 7-9.

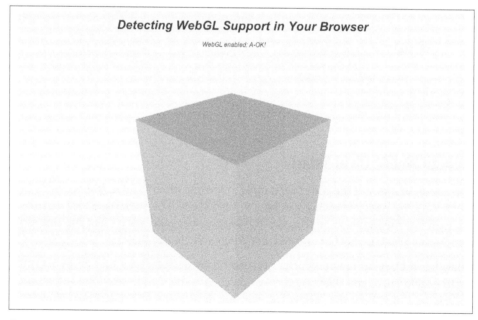

Figure 7-9. Browser detect result with WebGL enabled (Safari on Mac OS X)

Handling Context Lost Events

Another important tactic for making your WebGL application robust is the ability to handle extreme conditions in the graphics system. On some implementations and operating systems, access to the WebGL graphics system, including all memory buffers for vertices, textures, shaders, and such, can be completely lost to the application. In that state, any attempt to call a WebGL API will fail. This is known in WebGL parlance as a *lost context*. When the context is lost, all of your WebGL objects need to be re-created; in essence you have to redo all graphics initialization code. The browser tells you when the context has been lost, by sending a `webglcontextlost` DOM event from the canvas element.

There is an excellent write-up on the Khronos Group wiki about how to deal with this situation (*http://www.khronos.org/webgl/wiki/HandlingContextLost*). I created an example based on that. The example also uses a handy WebGL debugging utility written in JavaScript by Gregg Tavares of Google. This utility allows you to force a lost context by simulating it in code. This is a good thing to have, because it's actually pretty hard to make the browser lose the WebGL context just by clicking around, resizing windows, or switching applications. Note that there is nothing Three.js-specific in this technique; it can work equally well with any framework.

Run the example in file *Chapter 7/production-context-lost.html*. You will see a spinning, textured cube. Click anywhere in the content area and you can simulate the context lost event. You will see a status message come up below the heading on the page, telling you that it is handling the lost context and re-creating the graphics. See Figure 7-10.

The code that illustrates this technique can be found in the source file *Chapter 7/ contextLost.js*. This defines an application class, `ContextApp`, which simulates lost context and handles the event. Example 7-4 shows the code. The lines in boldface are ones to pay attention to. First, in the `init()` method we have to create a special wrapper for the canvas element, using the WebGL debugging utilities. That will allow us to force the context lost event so that we can reliably test this. Later on in `init()` we call a helper to add a DOM event listener for `webglcontextlost`. The method `addContextListen er()` shows the details for that. Finally, the code to handle the event is in method `handleContextLost()`. It is deceptively simple, namely we just re-create the canvas element and call our `init()` method again. But of course, the devil is in the details: you have to structure your code in such a way that `init()` can be called more than once without all hell breaking loose. Happy refactoring!

Example 7-4. Handling WebGL context lost

```
// Constructor
ContextApp = function()
{
    Sim.App.call(this);
}
```

*Figure 7-10. Detecting a lost WebGL context; rock texture created using Filter Forge (http://
filterforge.com/; license required for commercial use in your own projects)*

```
// Subclass Sim.App
ContextApp.prototype = new Sim.App();

// Our custom initializer
ContextApp.prototype.init = function(param)
{

    var debugCanvas =
    WebGLDebugUtils.makeLostContextSimulatingCanvas(document.createElement(
'canvas' ));

    param.canvas = debugCanvas;

    // Call superclass init code to set up scene, renderer, default camera
    Sim.App.prototype.init.call(this, param);

    // Create a light to show off the model
    var light = new THREE.DirectionalLight( 0xffffff, 1);
    light.position.set(0, 0, 1);
    this.scene.add(light);

    var amb = new THREE.AmbientLight( 0xffffff );
    this.scene.add(amb);
```

```
    this.camera.position.set(0, 0, 5);

    this.createModel();
    this.addContextListener();

    this.status = param.status;
}

ContextApp.prototype.update = function()
{
    Sim.App.prototype.update.call(this);
    this.mesh.rotation.y += 0.01;
}

ContextApp.prototype.createModel = function()
{
    // Create a few graphics objects to demonstrate re-creation on lost context
    var image = "../images/8890.jpg";
    var geometry = new THREE.CubeGeometry(2, 2, 2);
    var material = new THREE.MeshPhongMaterial({color:0xFFFFFF,
        map : THREE.ImageUtils.loadTexture(image)});

    var mesh = new THREE.Mesh(geometry, material);
    mesh.rotation.x = Math.PI / 6;
    mesh.rotation.y = Math.PI / 6;

    this.scene.add(mesh);

    this.mesh = mesh;
}

ContextApp.prototype.handleContextLost = function(e)
{
    // alert("Context lost! " + e);
    this.container.removeChild(this.renderer.domElement);
    this.status.innerHTML = "Context lost, re-initializing...";
    this.init( { container:this.container, status: this.status } );
    this.status.innerHTML += "done.";
}

ContextApp.prototype.addContextListener = function()
{
    var that = this;
    this.renderer.domElement.addEventListener("webglcontextlost",
            function(e) {
                that.handleContextLost(e);
                },
            false);
}

ContextApp.prototype.handleMouseDown = function(x, y)
```

```
{
    this.status.innerHTML = "";
    this.renderer.domElement.loseContext();
}
```

WebGL and Security

There is one final topic to cover to get through our gauntlet of WebGL production topics: security. WebGL is one of the new browser technologies that push the boundaries on features, getting pretty close to the metal of the machine. With that advance comes new potential for security flaws.

The browser developers implementing WebGL have worked extensively in the past few years to ensure that it is as secure as possible. This represents a mammoth effort that includes diligent conformance work within Khronos and the implementers, and outreach with standards groups and graphics chip manufacturers. There was even some drama around security and WebGL in 2010—some based on valid concerns around bugs in early releases—which now seems to have settled down.

The outcome of all this security work is largely behind the scenes for us web developers. However, one place where we need to pay attention is in the area of cross-domain (or *cross-origin*) programming. Let's say you want to create a texture map from an image on a website outside your own domain—for example, a photo shared on Flickr. If you were putting that image on an HTML page, no problem: simply create an <img> tag and the browser will show it. But with WebGL, that image is being painted on a <canvas> element, and the new and improved browser security restrictions prevent that without adding additional instrumentation to the web server serving up that image.

If you want to go old school, one way around the new cross-origin restrictions is to write an image proxy on your own server. This code downloads images from the other domain (e.g., using CURL in PHP), and then serves up the image data to your client. That eliminates the cross-origin situation, however at the expense of your own server bandwidth and processing time (which, on PHP at least, can be pretty darn slow).

A better and less crufty way to deal with cross-origin images is to employ Cross-Origin Resource Sharing, or CORS. CORS is a client-server mechanism whereby the server can accept or deny cross-origin requests. If a server accepts CORS requests (and responds to them favorably), you can fetch images and other resources from that domain. If you have experience developing applications with Adobe Flash, you may recognize this idea as being similar to the cross-domain policy file schema used with Flash (remember those *crossdomain.xml* files you always end up having to deal with on your server). CORS is a W3C initiative currently in working draft form, in modern browsers. It's not quite a standard, but it is on its way.

Understand that not all web servers support CORS. For example, if you try to grab that Flickr photo, the browser will throw up its hands because (as of this writing) Flickr won't allow the request. Other services will: Google Picasa allows anonymous CORS requests (i.e., coming from any domain by any user) for its images. Let's take a look at an example. Launch the file *Chapter 7/production-crossdomain-CORS.html*. You should see a picture of yours truly mapped onto a cube. That picture is hosted on Picasa. See Figure 7-11.

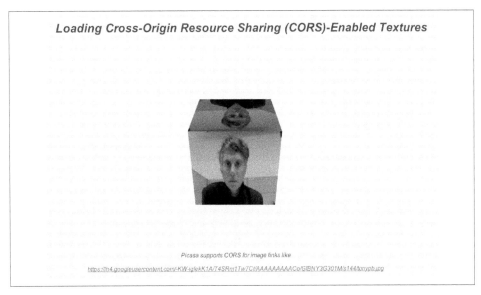

Figure 7-11. Using a Picasa photo as a texture

The client-side code for making a CORS-compliant request is quite straightforward. Before making an image fetch by setting the `src` property of an `Image` element, first set its `crossOrigin` property. Let's have a look at some code from source file *Chapter 7/ CORSImageApp.js*, listed in Example 7-5.

Example 7-5. CORS request code for Image element
```
CORSImageApp.prototype.createModel = function()
{
    // Load image with valid Picasa url
    var image ='https://lh4.googleusercontent.com/-KW-igfekK1A/' +
        'T4SRm1Tw7CI/AAAAAAAACo/GIBNY3G301M/s144/tonypb.jpg';

    var that = this;

    var img = new Image();
    img.crossOrigin = ''; // synonymous with, er, 'anonymous'
    img.onload = function(){

        // Create a new Three.js texture with this image, flag needs update
        var texture = new THREE.Texture(img);
        texture.needsUpdate = true;
```

```
// Drop the map image onto a cube, easy-peasy
var geometry = new THREE.CubeGeometry(1, 1, 1);
var material = new THREE.MeshPhongMaterial({color:0xFFFFFF, map:
texture});

var mesh = new THREE.Mesh(geometry, material);
mesh.rotation.x = Math.PI / 6;
mesh.rotation.y = Math.PI /6;

that.scene.add(mesh);

that.mesh = mesh;
};

img.src = image;
}
```

Our application's createModel() method fetches a Picasa image before creating any geometry. That part is done in the callback, once we know we have an image. Before doing the fetch, we set img.crossOrigin to an empty string, which is synonymous with the value 'anonymous'. We then add an onload callback function, and fetch the image. Once the image arrives, our callback creates a Three.js texture using the Image element. Without the cross-origin support in place, any attempt to do this will generate an exception from the browser. With it in place, it works like a charm. It's great that Google is out in front on CORS support on its servers; it will be better still when other popular services support it as well.

Chapter Summary

This chapter tackled a big range of topics, from content creation to security. I know it ranged far and wide, but the material should put us in a place where we feel comfortable going forth and building real applications, not just kicking the tires on a new graphics technology.

First, we took a step back and thought about frameworks. I am a big fan of Three.js, but the world of WebGL is bigger than that, and you might need to look elsewhere for something that meets your needs. Then, we dug into the details of 3D file formats and took a peek at a few tools for creating content. Finally, things got really real as we covered issues related to making robust and secure WebGL applications.

Now that we're fully up and running, it's time to step on the gas. In the next chapter, we're going to build a game.

CHAPTER 8

Your First WebGL Game

The stage is set; we have the bits and pieces required to develop a WebGL application. We know how to render graphics, and bring life to them with animations and interactivity. We learned how to integrate 2D HTML5 elements with our 3D content, making for a seamless user experience. We kicked the tires on tools for creating 3D models and scenes, and explored techniques for building robustness into our WebGL code. It's time to put all this working knowledge together. Let's build our first game!

Figure 8-1 depicts the game. It's a car race, and the rules are simple: (1) Go as fast as you can, and (2) don't crash into the other cars. You speed along a straight stretch of desert road located on the Californian leg of the legendary Route 66, avoiding any cars ahead of you. If you get too close to the guardrail, you will bounce around and lose time. In the background, clouds slowly move against a desert blue sky. A heads-up display shows a readout of your current speed, engine RPM, elapsed time, and distance. At the end of the race, an overlay appears, showing the final result and inviting you to play again.

I chose this game theme more or less at random…though I did try to pick a genre that would illustrate all the key concepts. I also wanted to identify something that I could create on my own using free and/or inexpensive stock art. The game is simple, but it gets the point across. It's also fun to play—for two or three minutes, anyway.

The racing game pulls together lessons we have learned up to now into a working application. To develop it, we will review the following concepts from earlier chapters:

Graphics
> Using Three.js primitive shapes to render the environment art (ground, sky, road)

Models
> Converting polygonal models (cars and road signs) from popular formats to the Three.js JSON format for loading into the game

Figure 8-1. A WebGL racing game (see the Examples README file for texture map and model credits)

Animation

Using the Sim.js keyframe utilities to animate car behaviors (turn, bump, crash), and programmatically animating textures to create a moving road and sky background

2D/3D integration

Exploiting WebGL's powerful compositing to create a heads-up display (HUD) with a speedometer, tachometer, time clock, and trip odometer

Building a robust WebGL application

Incorporating browser detection and context lost event handling to make the game behave properly under adverse conditions

To create a polished game, we will also tackle a few new subjects:

Effects

Creating a particle system to achieve a smoke effect for the car exhaust

Keyboard input

Driving the car using keys on the keyboard

Sound

Adding sound to a WebGL application for realism

A lot goes into building a game, even a simple demo like this. Game development covers a wide range of topics, well beyond the scope of this book. Inevitably, we will give short shrift to important issues related to game design, engine development, art direction, and production. But we will at least touch on those ideas throughout the chapter. Let's get into it.

Building the Pieces

In its early stages, game development tends to be exploratory and proceeds in small steps. Art takes a central, rather than supportive, role; engineering is often pushing the bleeding edge to get that one novel special effect. Good game development teams build a series of prototypes and studies before nailing down a production plan and fully committing resources.

In that spirit, we have organized our work into several small projects; think of them as prototypes, or labs. Each one answers a set of key questions around interaction, art, design, and technology, and also represents a milestone toward the completion of the project. Much of the lab work can be reused directly, or with slight modification, within the finished project. But it is really the learning that counts.

Camera, Character, and Control

My friend Scott Foe (*http://scottfoe.blogspot.com/*) is a game industry veteran, a game designer extraordinaire, and possibly the best producer on the planet. Scott has drilled it into me that the absolute first step in building any video game is to establish "3CAD." 3CAD stands for Character, Camera, Control, and Art Direction: define the world, the character's identity, his point of view, and how he moves within the world. Once you have locked those down you can proceed with designing your play elements, material, win conditions, mechanics, and so on. But it all starts with 3CAD.

For the racing game, I tackled 3CAD in two stages: first, the Character, Camera, and Control. Figure 8-2 shows what some game developers call a "Gray Box" prototype. It implements the Character, which in the case of our racing game is actually the car; it establishes a Camera point of view, specifically a "third person" or over-the-shoulder view; and it provides Controls for moving the car down the road, in this case, the arrow keys on the keyboard. Launch the file *Chapter 8/game-graybox.html* to try it out.

Figure 8-2. "Gray Box" prototype for character, camera, and control

In the Gray Box prototype, the three Cs are implemented in detail: the car is fully rendered, down to the particle system used for the exhaust; the keyboard controls work as they are intended within the game; and all behaviors, such as the simplistic physics used to detect car collisions and the animations for the car crash, are present. Even the texture animation for the road (discussed shortly) is in there because it provides critical visual cues about the car's speed and hence the functioning of the keyboard controls. In contrast, all nonessential elements are rendered with placeholders—such as boxes for the cars and geometry without textures—or they are omitted altogether.

The goal of the Gray Box prototype is to understand the character we are building and how it relates to the world. It is essential for getting a sense of how the game will "feel." But it also has the pragmatic benefit of telling us very early in the process—right at step 1—if we need to invest more in certain aspects of development. We may discover unexpected things when playing with the prototype—for example, that we need a figure-eight track instead of a straight one; or that the basic distance-based collision doesn't feel right and therefore we need to build in real physics.

Let's take a look at a few snippets of code from the Gray Box prototype. We'll see some familiar stuff as well as a few new ideas. The Gray Box application code can be found in source file *Chapter 8/grayBox.js*.

The keyboard controls

One of the great things about WebGL is that you don't need to learn a whole new application platform to create 3D; the platform is the web browser. To add keyboard support to your WebGL application, simply add DOM event handlers to the canvas element. Sim.js sets this up already, so our game just needs to implement the methods handleKeyUp() and handleKeyDown() and we're good to go.

In the Gray Box prototype, the application dispatches key up and key down events to the Player object (source file *Chapter 8/player.js*). See Example 8-1.

Example 8-1. Keyboard handling in the Player object

```
Player.prototype.handleKeyDown = function(keyCode, charCode)
{
    this.keysDown[keyCode] = true;
}

Player.prototype.handleKeyUp = function(keyCode, charCode)
{
    this.keysDown[keyCode] = false;
}
```

The Player object maintains an array of keys being pressed in the keysDown property. In its update() method, it will inspect that array see if it needs to move. Example 8-2 shows an excerpt from Player.update(). If the left arrow key is held down, the car turns left; if the right arrow key is held down, it turns right. If neither of those is held down, the car is straightened out. update() also handles accelerating the car: the up arrow speeds it up; the down arrow slows it down. If neither up nor down is pressed, the car coasts, naturally slowing down a bit.

Example 8-2. Keyboard handling in the Update method

```
var turning = false;
if (this.keysDown[Sim.KeyCodes.KEY_LEFT])
{
    this.turn(-0.1);
    turning = true;
}

if (this.keysDown[Sim.KeyCodes.KEY_RIGHT])
{
    this.turn(0.1);
    turning = true;
}

if (!turning)
{
    this.turn(0);
}

if (this.keysDown[Sim.KeyCodes.KEY_UP])
```

```
{
    this.accelerate(0.02);
}
else if (this.keysDown[Sim.KeyCodes.KEY_DOWN])
{
    this.accelerate(-0.02);
}
else
{
    this.accelerate(-0.01);
}
```

Note the key code values such as `Sim.KeyCodes.KEY_LEFT`. These are defined in Sim.js as follows:

```
Sim.KeyCodes = {};
Sim.KeyCodes.KEY_LEFT  = 37;
Sim.KeyCodes.KEY_UP    = 38;
Sim.KeyCodes.KEY_RIGHT = 39;
Sim.KeyCodes.KEY_DOWN  = 40;
```

You might be wondering where those values came from. After some hunting online, I dug up the key codes for the arrow keys. It's interesting—amazing, really—that in this day and age, key codes are still not guaranteed to be cross-browser, or standardized by W3C. However, modern browsers appear to have converged on their interpretation of common key codes and the ones in the preceding code snippet worked in the browsers I tested. I found a couple of websites with more information on key codes: *http://www.javascripter.net/faq/keycodes.htm* and *http://www.cambiaresearch.com/articles/15/javascript-char-codes-key-codes*. I suppose the moral is, tread carefully when writing keyboard support in your browser-based games.

The camera

We haven't really played with the camera very much in this book. We typically set an initial position and forget it. But with our racing game, we need to move the camera along with the car. Let's look into how that's done.

The `Player` object is responsible for tracking the player's car with the camera. The natural place to do this is—where else?—in the `update()` method. After the turns and accelerations have been handled, `update()` calls the helper method `updateCamera()`. Let's have a look at what it does in Example 8-3.

Example 8-3. Updating the camera

```
Player.prototype.updateCamera = function()
{
    var camerapos = new THREE.Vector3(Player.CAMERA_OFFSET_X,
            Player.CAMERA_OFFSET_Y, Player.CAMERA_OFFSET_Z);
    camerapos.addSelf(this.object3D.position);
    this.camera.position.copy(camerapos);
    this.camera.lookAt(this.object3D.position);
```

`updateCamera()` maintains a constant offset and viewing angle, so we always see the car from the same point of view as it moves. First, we set up a vector with predefined *x*, *y*, and *z* offsets. That vector is then added to the car's position using the Three.js vector's `addSelf()` method. We then move the camera by copying that value to the camera's position. That moves the camera, but we need to make sure it continues to point at the car; the camera's `lookAt()` method takes care of that. This is a really useful method of the camera object: wherever the camera is, you simply pass it a position to look at, and it will reorient itself.

Keyframe animations

The Gray Box prototype requires animation to provide a complete Camera, Character, and Control experience. We need to see how the character responds when we move, and when we collide with the guardrails or crash into other cars; for that we need some animations.

Source file *Chapter 8/car.js* contains the code for the car animations. Let's have a look at the creation code and keyframe data for the crash animation in Example 8-4.

Example 8-4. Crash animation code and keyframe data

```
Car.prototype.createCrashAnimation = function()
{
    this.crashAnimator = new Sim.KeyFrameAnimator;
    this.crashAnimator.init({
        interps:
            [
            { keys:Car.crashPositionKeys,
                values:Car.crashPositionValues,
                target:this.mesh.position },
            { keys:Car.crashRotationKeys,
                values:Car.crashRotationValues,
                target:this.mesh.rotation }
            ],
        loop: false,
        duration:Car.crash_animation_time
    });

    this.addChild(this.crashAnimator);
    this.crashAnimator.subscribe("complete", this,
        this.onCrashAnimationComplete);
}

Car.prototype.animateCrash = function(on)
{
    if (on)
    {
        this.crashAnimator.start();
    }
    else
```

```
        {
            this.crashAnimator.stop();
        }
    }
}

Car.prototype.onCrashAnimationComplete = function()
{
}

...

Car.crashPositionKeys = [0, .25, .75, 1];
Car.crashPositionValues = [ { x : -1, y: 0, z : 0},
                            { x: 0, y: 1, z: -1},
                            { x: 1, y: 0, z: -5},
                            { x : -1, y: 0, z : -2}
                            ];
Car.crashRotationKeys = [0, .25, .5, .75, 1];
Car.crashRotationValues = [ { z: 0, y: 0 },
                            { z: Math.PI, y: 0},
                            { z: Math.PI * 2, y: 0},
                            { z: Math.PI * 2, y: Math.PI},
                            { z: Math.PI * 2, y: Math.PI * 2},
                            ];

Car.crash_animation_time = 2000;
```

When we detect a collision between our player car and one of the other cars, we call
animateCrash(true) and the animation plays. There is similar code and keyframe data
for the bounce animation that is triggered when the player car collides with a guardrail.
Note that the Player object inherits from Car, and so all cars share the code and keyframes for animating crashes and bounces.

Texture animation

There is one other important animation to cover in our prototype: the road texture.
Rather than model the road geometry to its actual length of 2 kilometers to the finish
line, we have modeled it with a length of 400 meters to give ourselves a smaller, more
manageable environment to work in. During play, the cars move more slowly than is
apparent so that it takes some time to get to the finish line. But because we are animating
the road texture map's *y* offset at twice the rate of the cars' movement along the road, it
appears that the cars are moving much faster. Example 8-5 shows the code, from the
Environment object's update() method (source file *Chapter 8/environment.js*).

Example 8-5. Code to animate the road texture
```
Environment.prototype.update = function()
{
    if (this.textureSky)
    {
        this.sky.material.map.offset.x += 0.00005;
```

```
    }

    if (this.app.running)
    {
        var now = Date.now();
        var deltat = now - this.curTime;
        this.curTime = now;

        dist = -deltat / 1000 * this.app.player.speed;
        this.road.material.map.offset.y +=
            (dist * Environment.ANIMATE_ROAD_FACTOR);
    }

    Sim.Object.prototype.update.call(this);
}
```

This is a pretty popular technique, and one of my all-time favorite game hacks. The speed that the cars move against the road is slower than the apparent speed, because we can trick the eye with a quickly moving texture map. To see just how tricky this effect is, comment out the two lines in boldface, run the prototype again, and watch how slowly the cars seem to move.

Collision detection

This game wouldn't be a challenge without the risk of running into other cars. We need to implement *collision detection* to tell us when our player gets too close to another car, or hits a guardrail. In a more complicated game, we would use a physics engine for this, either off-the-shelf or one of our own design. A physics engine would let us define velocity, acceleration, and other physical properties of each car, the road, the guardrails, and so on, and compute collisions between objects every frame.

But this game is pretty simple: we only have to test colliding against the sides of a straight road, and against one of five cars. So we are going to write the code ourselves. Example 8-6 shows the code for GrayBox.testCollision() in its entirety.

Example 8-6. Collision detection in the Gray Box prototype
```
GrayBox.prototype.testCollision = function()
{
    var playerpos = this.player.object3D.position;

    if (playerpos.x > (Environment.ROAD_WIDTH / 2 - (Car.CAR_WIDTH/2)))
    {
        this.player.bounce();
        this.player.object3D.position.x -= 1;
    }

    if (playerpos.x < -(Environment.ROAD_WIDTH / 2 - (Car.CAR_WIDTH/2)))
    {
        this.player.bounce();
        this.player.object3D.position.x += 1;
```

```
        }

        var i, len = this.cars.length;
        for (i = 0; i < len; i++)
        {
            var carpos = this.cars[i].object3D.position;
            var dist = playerpos.distanceTo(carpos);
            if (dist < GrayBox.COLLIDE_RADIUS)
            {
                this.player.crash();
                this.cars[i].crash();
                this.running = false;
                break;
            }
        }
    }
}
```

The collision check against the guardrails is quite simple: just test the car's *x* position to make sure it is within the bounds of the road. With a straight piece of road, there's nothing to it. As for the collision against other cars, that is less trivial but nonetheless pretty easy. We loop through the other cars, testing to see if the player is closer than the predefined collision radius. If it is, that means we have crashed. See the line of code in boldface: it uses the Three.js `Vector3` class method `distanceTo()`, which calculates the Euclidean distance to another vector.

Again, this game is so simple that this was all the collision code we needed. For information on physics engines that support sophisticated collision for WebGL, see Appendix A.

That's it for the Gray Box prototype. We like our camera, character, and control, and we feel good about the animated effects and collisions. Now it's time for the art direction.

Art Direction

Art Direction—the second part of 3CAD—is an equally necessary step in understanding your game. It is an opportunity to establish your visual parameters and answer key questions: what kind of look are you going for—future or retro? What kind of mood—whimsical or dark? What style—realistic or cartoony? Are you targeting a male or female audience, or a certain age demographic?

Art Direction will also flush out production and technical issues. For example, you may think you can get away with procedurally generated trees to save development dollars, but when you put them in your art direction prototype you discover that they really don't cut it. Or maybe you assumed that you could use traditional rendering for an effect, only to find that you really need to invest some programmer time in a custom shader to get that look you're going for.

Figure 8-3 shows a screenshot of the art direction study (file *Chapter 8/game-art-direction.html*). Here we have included all of the important visual elements: all objects are textured; the car exhaust is in there to provide a sense of the mood; our Route 66 road signs are in place, dividing the space visually; we have a textured finish line sign (made by yours truly using free tools at *http://www.sumopaint.com*); and we have dropped in the heads-up display and the end screen to make sure that they complement the visual style of the scene. We included the keyboard handling from the Gray Box prototype in order to move around the scene, but this is only for the purpose of exploring the art (i.e., making sure it looks OK from all camera points of view). Anything not directly related to these issues is faked or omitted: the HUD controls and end screen are populated with random values; and there is no collision against the other cars or the guardrails, so you can wander off-road.

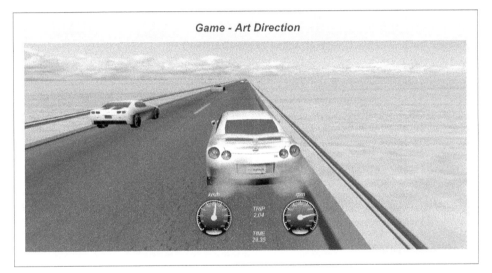

Figure 8-3. Art direction study for the game

The sky background

The sky is another cheap trick, just a wide rectangle placed far out at the edge of the world where the player can't ever reach. The moving clouds use the texture offset animation technique from Example 8-5: the first few lines of `Environment.update()` scroll the sky texture in the *x* dimension. In this case I was a bit lazy and simply offset the texture *x* coordinate by a fixed amount each frame, rather than calculating the offset as a function of time.

The heads-up display

The HUD controls are a great example of how important 2D/3D compositing is for WebGL. Not only can we deliver a seamless user experience, but also, because we are developing our HUD with HTML5, I was able to find an open source speedometer control that I could just drop in. You can get Marcello Barnaba's speedometer widget at *https://github.com/vjt/canvas-speedometer*. It's awesome, easy to use, and fully customizable. Kudos and thanks, Marcello!

Changing textures on the fly

Finally, we played a few tricks with the car models. Looking around on TurboSquid I only found a couple of usable models for the nonplayer cars, a Chevy Nova and a Camaro. But by simply swapping textures we can make it look like there are more types of cars in the scene. The Camaro model came in a ZIP file that included a variety of textures. After Three.js loads the model from the JSON file, which specifies the URL to the default yellow texture, our code swaps that texture out for the silver one. Example 8-7 has the code, from file *Chapter 8/artDirection.js*.

Example 8-7. Code to change textures on the fly

```
ArtDirection.prototype.createCar = function(makeIndex)
{
    var model = this.carModels[makeIndex].model;
    var options = this.carModels[makeIndex].options;

    var group = new THREE.Object3D;
    group.rotation.y = Math.PI;

    var mesh = new THREE.Mesh(model.mesh.geometry, model.mesh.material);
    mesh.rotation.set(options.rotation.x,
        options.rotation.y, options.rotation.z)
    mesh.scale.set(options.scale, options.scale, options.scale);
    mesh.position.set(options.position.x,
        options.position.y, options.position.z);

    if (options.map)
    {
        var material = mesh.geometry.materials[options.mapIndex];
        material.map = THREE.ImageUtils.loadTexture(options.map);
    }

    group.add(mesh);

    return group;
}
```

First, we load the cars in the usual way, using the JSONModel class. Once we have detected that all of our models are loaded, we call the createCar() helper method in a loop. This method makes a new mesh based on the geometry and materials loaded by the JSON loader. There is also an `options` object stored for each car make; this has the information about scale, position, and rotation to apply, as well as whether to swap textures. All of these are applied to the mesh before the car is added to the scene. The lines of code in bold show how the texture is swapped by setting the `map` property of the mesh's material.

The Model Previewer

The models loaded into our scene—the player car, nonplayer cars, and the road signs— each require a bit of manipulation after being loaded. We just saw how to change the texture on the Camaro models to give the illusion of different cars. But we also may need to change the models in other ways. You never know what you are getting with stock art: coordinate systems, units, normals, and so on may have to be changed to get them game-ready. Rather than load each model into the finished art scene on a trial-and-error basis, it would be better to use a simple tool to preview each model and find the issues.

To that end, we have adapted the model viewer from the preceding chapter. The new version provides information we'll need for the game. Figure 8-4 depicts the viewer after loading our player car. Check it out by loading *Chapter 8/game-model-viewer.html* into your browser.

Figure 8-4. Model previewer for game assets

Choose one of the options in the select box. When the model loads, note the DIV element on the upper right: it displays the dimensions of the model (width, height, and depth).

It also reports the number of materials and the number of polygons (faces) it found in the mesh. Let's have a quick look at the code for figuring that out. Example 8-8 shows the code for onModelLoaded(), a callback function defined in the HTML file. This function is called when the JSON model loading is complete.

Example 8-8. Callback handler for JSON model loader

```
function onModelLoaded(model, info)
{
    var geometry = model.mesh.geometry;

    // Display the bounding box, number of materials and
    number of faces
    geometry.computeBoundingBox();
    var bbox = geometry.boundingBox;
    var width = bbox.x[1] - bbox.x[0];
    var height = bbox.y[1] - bbox.y[0];
    var depth = bbox.z[1] - bbox.z[0];

    var nMaterials = geometry.materials.length;
    var nFaces = geometry.faces.length;
    var nPlaces = 3;

    var statsHTML = "Model Info<br>Dimensions: " +
        width.toFixed(nPlaces) + " x " +
        height.toFixed(nPlaces) + " x " +
        depth.toFixed(nPlaces) +
        "<br># Materials: " + nMaterials +
        "<br># Faces: " + nFaces;

    info.model = model;
    info.stats = statsHTML;

    displayModelStats(statsHTML);
}
```

Note the lines in boldface. The Three.js `Geometry` object has a method for computing its *bounding box* (i.e., its maximum width, height, and depth based on its vertex values). We also use this callback to fetch information about the geometry's materials and number of polygons. All of this is reported via a DIV element popped up on the upper right.

This is great information to have. For the Nissan model, we discover that the dimensions of the car are 84.140 × 55.456 × 182.712. You may well be wondering, in what units? At first it's not obvious, and there is no metadata in the original OBJ file or converted JSON to tell us. I ended up going online, and discovered that this particular car is 4.6 meters long in the real world. That turns out to be 182 inches, so this model is accurately modeled in inches. Armed with that knowledge, we can scale the model by 0.0254 to make the conversion to meters. (I found that on Google, too.)

In doing this for all the models in the scene, my results varied wildly. The Nissan at least was modeled accurately in real-world units. But for some of the models, the units seemed arbitrary and not connected to the real world. Some were modeled with the y- and z-axes flipped, or their pivot points off-center, and so on. So there was quite a bit of experimentation with the position, rotation, and scale values within the previewer code. That's life in the fast line using free art: you often get what you pay for. Anyway, eventually I was able to find reasonable scale values for each object, which I then dropped into the art direction study for a sanity check, and ultimately used in the game.

 In a real game project, we would have a "level editor" (i.e., some kind of visual development environment) to sort all this out. Even for this simple game I would have liked to have a better tool, one that let me interactively inspect parts of the model, report the texture information, maybe rescale the model into different units and save it out to a new file. Perhaps some enterprising soul will build a good level editor for WebGL soon (hint, hint).

Creating a Particle System

The exhaust spewing from the rear of the car represents the finishing touch on art direction. In my opinion this makes the game; the car feels so much more real with the exhaust than without. If you recall back to Chapter 3, we utilized the Three.js built-in `ParticleSystem` object to render stars for the solar system. But that was a different kind of particle system. It was a static object consisting of WebGL point primitives. To get the smoke effect required for exhaust fumes, we are going to create a dynamic particle system composed of texture-mapped polygons, and animate each particle each frame. Figure 8-5 shows the particle system prototype (file *Chapter 8/game-particles.html*).

The code to create and animate the particle system is pretty straightforward. However, it took me a lot of experimentation to get the exact effect I wanted, where the smoke appears to rise as well as billow. Let's have a look at the listing in Example 8-9. Our class `Exhaust` has methods `initParticles()` and `update()` to create and animate the particles, respectively. See source file *Chapter 8/exhaust.js*.

Example 8-9. Creating and animating the particle system

```
Exhaust.prototype.initParticles = function()
{
    var sphereRadius = 1;

    var particleCount = 100;
    var particles = new THREE.Geometry();


    var pMaterial = new THREE.ParticleBasicMaterial({
            color: 0xffffff,
```

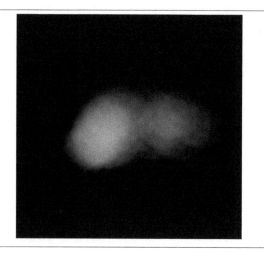

Figure 8-5. Particle system prototype

```
        size: 1,
        opacity:.05,
        transparent:true,
        map: new THREE.ImageUtils.loadTexture(
            '../images/smoke-2.png')
    });


for(var p = 0; p < particleCount; p++) {

    var radius =  sphereRadius*0.05;
    var angle = Math.random() * (Math.PI * 2)
    var pX = Math.sin(angle) * radius,
        pY = Math.random() * 1,
        pZ = 0,
        particle = new THREE.Vertex(
            new THREE.Vector3(pX, pY, pZ)
        );

    particle.velocity = new THREE.Vector3(
        Math.random()-0.5,                // x
        Math.random()*0.25,    // y
        0);                 // z

    particles.vertices.push(particle);
}

// create the particle system
var particleSystem = new THREE.ParticleSystem(
    particles,
    pMaterial);
```

```
    particleSystem.position.y = sphereRadius*-0.2;

    particleSystem.sortParticles = false;

    // add it to the scene
    this.object3D.add(particleSystem);

    this.particleCount = particleCount;
    this.particles = particles;
    this.particleSystem = particleSystem;
    this.sphereRadius = sphereRadius;
}

Exhaust.prototype.update = function()
{
    //update particles
    var pCount = this.particleCount;
    while(pCount--) {

        var particle = this.particles.vertices[pCount];

        if(particle.position.y > .25 || particle.position.y < 0) {
            particle.position.y = 0;
            var radius =  this.sphereRadius*0.05;
            var angle = Math.random() * (Math.PI * 2);
            particle.position.x = Math.cos(angle) * radius;
        }

        //continue;

        var t = Date.now() / 1000 % 3;
        particle.position.x += Math.cos(t*particle.velocity.x) * .007;
        particle.position.y += Math.sin(t*particle.velocity.y) * .05;

    }
    this.particleSystem.geometry.__dirtyVertices = true;
}
```

Three.js uses a special material type, THREE.ParticleBasicMaterial, to render particles. (Recall that each material type in Three.js corresponds to a WebGL shader.) We
create one of those, supplying a particle size, color, opacity value, and texture map. The
texture is just a single puff of smoke—but the particle system we are about to create is
going to have 100 of those animating wildly. Using transparency, these will blend beautifully into a cloud of smoke.

Next, we create the particles themselves. That is just a THREE.Geometry object populated
with vertices for which we generate a random position in *x* and *y* (the *z* coordinate will

remain 0). We also give each one a random velocity in x and y. Once we have the material and geometry, we can create the `ParticleSystem` and add it to the simulation just like any other 3D object. (We actually add two particle systems as children of the player car: one for the left exhaust and one for the right.)

`update()` animates the particle system: looping through the particles one by one, it generates a new position based on the particle's initial velocity vector. It clamps all the values within a given range so that particles don't fly off into space; we only have a fixed set of particles, so we have to recycle them when they get too far away.

Note that the Three.js `ParticleSystem` is pretty limited compared to those found in popular game engines. Typically particle systems have built-in physics models for wind, gravity, and such, and can spawn an indefinite number of objects rather than needing to recycle them. Still, this one was pretty easy to use, and it got the job done: the effect turned out great.

Adding Sound

Before we are ready to assemble the game, we need to tackle one final topic: sound. Some games—I would argue, most—require sound, and others don't. If you think your game needs sound, don't leave it until the last minute. Get your sound design together early; it can make all the difference. I can't imagine a racing game without road sounds, tire squeals, and a car crash or two. So let's make some noise!

Launch *Chapter 8/game-sounds.html* to open the sound lab. You should see a page that looks like Figure 8-6.

The sound lab uses the HTML5 `<audio>` tag to embed sounds in the HTML. This is a dead simple page containing multiple audio elements, plus buttons and sliders to control their parameters.

The point of the lab is twofold: (1) provide a simple interface for testing and mixing the sounds, and (2) experiment with the HTML5 audio element's API so that we know how to control the sounds in game. Try it out: click the play/pause controls and experiment with the other controls in the built-in audio UI. Try starting more than one sound, to get a feel for how they will mix during game time. Then, try the individual buttons and sliders; those are controls I added which flex the audio API, because that is what we will be using in the game.

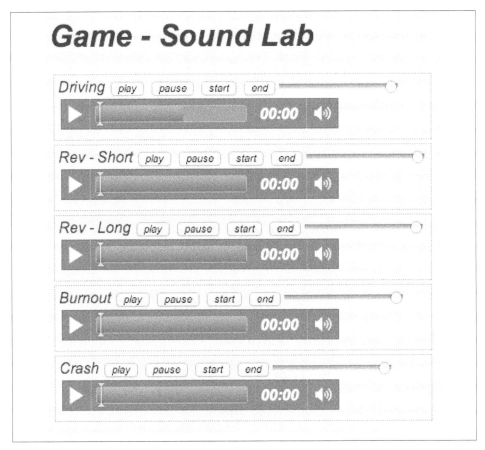

Figure 8-6. Sound lab for game sound design

 I downloaded the sound files for the game from Freesound, a great sound-sharing site (*http://www.freesound.org*). After a little editing using WavePad they were ready to go (you can download a free 30-day WavePad trial at *http://www.nch.com.au/wavepad/index.html*). Another great free, open source tool for sound editing is Audacity (*http:// audacity.sourceforge.net/*), which boasts support for several HTML5-friendly audio formats, including Ogg Vorbis and MP3.

The HTML audio element is perfect for putting simple sound into your game. It is easy to use and provides basic controls: you can start, stop, pause, and seek; and it tells you when enough data has arrived so that the sound is ready to play. It's certainly good enough for our purposes here. However, many games require more precise audio control: sub-mixing, special effects, spatialization (i.e., moving the sound around in 3D), and so on. There are other, more powerful audio APIs being shipped in today's browsers.

Unfortunately, none of them have been standardized as of this writing. For more information, have a look at Google's Web Audio specification (*https://dvcs.w3.org/hg/audio/raw-file/tip/webaudio/specification.html*), a W3C draft, and Mozilla's Audio Data API at *https://wiki.mozilla.org/Audio_Data_API*.

Putting It All Together

It's time to put the game together. We feel good about the controls and interaction; the art direction is solid; we cobbled together a tool to help prepare models; and we figured out some nice effects and sound design. Because we have been building the pieces as we go, at this point, it's largely an assembly job.

There are still a few things to do. We have to wire up the HUD controls to the real speed, RPM, elapsed time, and distance. We're also going to add a little polish, in the form of the end screen with a Restart button inviting the user to play again. Finally, we want to make sure the game is reliable and robust, so we should deal with browser detection and context lost, as we learned about in the preceding chapter. The final result is depicted in Figure 8-7. Launch the file *Chapter 8/game.html* and try it out. Happy racing!

Figure 8-7. The finished game

The full code listings for the HTML file, and the game engine source in *Chapter 8/game.js*, can be found in Examples 8-10 and 8-11.

Example 8-10. HTML source for racing game
```
<!DOCTYPE html>
<html>
<head>
```

```
<title>Road Race!</title>

    <link href="../css/webglbook.css" rel="stylesheet" />
    <link rel="stylesheet" type="text/css" href="game.css" />
    <script src="../libs/Three.js"></script>
    <script src="../libs/jquery-1.6.4.js"></script>
    <script src="../libs/jquery.mousewheel.js"></script>
    <script src="../libs/RequestAnimationFrame.js"></script>
    <script src="../sim/sim.js"></script>
    <script src="../sim/animation.js"></script>
    <script src="../sim/webGLDetector.js"></script>
    <script src="jsonModel.js"></script>
    <script src="car.js"></script>
    <script src="player.js"></script>
    <script src="exhaust.js"></script>
    <script src="environment.js"></script>
    <script src="game.js"></script>
    <script type="text/javascript" src="xcanvas.js"></script>
    <script type="text/javascript" src="tbe.js"></script>

    <script type="text/javascript" src="digitaldisplay.js"></script>
    <script type="text/javascript" src="speedometer.js"></script>
    <script type="text/javascript" src="themes/default.js"></script>
    <script type="text/javascript" src="themes/racing-black.js"></script>
    <script>

    // Awesome speedometer code - here's the source!
    // https://github.com/vjt/canvas-speedometer

    var game_volume = 1;

    function loadSounds()
    {
        var sounds = {
            driving : document.getElementById ('driving'),
            rev_short : document.getElementById ('rev_short'),
            rev_long : document.getElementById ('rev_long'),
            bounce : document.getElementById ('bounce'),
            crash : document.getElementById ('crash'),
        };

        return sounds;
    }

    function adjustVolume(sounds, volume)
    {
        for (sound in sounds)
        {
            sounds[sound].volume = volume;
        }
    }
```

```
var app = null;

$(document).ready(
    function() {

        var container = document.getElementById("container");

        try {

            Sim.WebGLDetector.detectWebGL();

            var timer = document.getElementById ('elapsedTime');
            var odometer = document.getElementById ('odometer');
            var kmph = document.getElementById ('kmph');
            var rpm = document.getElementById ('rpm');

            var sounds = loadSounds();
            adjustVolume(sounds, game_volume);

            // Check out configuration and API on GitHub Wiki:
            // http://wiki.github.com/vjt/canvas-speedometer
            speedometer = new Speedometer (
                'speedometer',{theme: 'racing-black', max:250,
                threshold:150});
            speedometer.draw ();
            speedometer.addEventListener (
                'speedometer:animateend', function () {
              controls.start ();
            });

            // The tachometer
            tachometer = new Speedometer ('tachometer',
                {theme: 'racing-black', max:5000,
                threshold:3500});
            tachometer.draw();
            tachometer.addEventListener (
                'speedometer:animateend', function () {
              tachcontrols.start ();
            });


            app = new RacingGame();
            app.init({ container: container,
                hud: {
                    speedometer:speedometer,
                    tachometer:tachometer,
                    timer:timer,
                    odometer:odometer,
                    },
                sounds : sounds,
            });
```

```
                    timer.style.display = 'block';
                    odometer.style.display = 'block';
                    kmph.style.display = 'block';
                    rpm.style.display = 'block';

                    app.focus();
                    app.run();

                }
                catch(e)
                {
                    container.innerHTML = e.toString();
                }
            }
        }
    );

    function onRestartClicked()
    {
        app.restart();
    }

    </script>

</head>
<body>
    <center><h1>Road Race!</h1></center>
    <!--
        Sky background texture
        http://freestocktextures.com/texture/id/557
      -->
    <div id="container"></div>
    <div id="kmph">
    km/h
        <div id="speedometer"></div>
    </div>
    <div id="rpm">
    rpm
        <div id="tachometer"></div>
    </div>
    <div id="odometer">
    0.00
    </div>
    <div id="elapsedTime">
    0.00
    </div>
    <div id="overlay" class="overlay" >
    <div id="header" class="header">RACE COMPLETE</div>
    <div id="contents" class="contents">
    ELAPSED TIME: 42.43s<br></br>
    BEST TIME: 39.31s
    </div>
      <div id="restartButton" class="restartButton">
```

```
            <button onclick="onRestartClicked(this);">Restart
            </button>
        </div>
    </div>

<!-- Sound credits -->
<!--

Driving in a Car
http://www.freesound.org/people/RutgerMuller/sounds/50910/
Nissan Maxima Burnout
http://www.freesound.org/people/audible-edge/sounds/71740/
Car Crash http://www.freesound.org/people/sandyrb/sounds/95078/
Car Revving http://www.freesound.org/people/Walter_Odington/sounds/18620/
 -->

    <audio id="driving">
      <source
        src="../sounds/50910__rutgermuller__in-car-driving.wav"
        type="audio/wav" />
      Your browser does not support WAV files in the audio element.
    </audio>
    <audio id="rev_short">
      <source src="../sounds/rev-short.wav" type="audio/wav" />
      Your browser does not support WAV files in the audio element.
    </audio>
    <audio id="rev_long">
      <source src="../sounds/rev-trimmed.wav" type="audio/wav" />
      Your browser does not support WAV files in the audio element.
    </audio>
    <audio id="bounce">
      <source src="../sounds/bounce.wav" type="audio/wav" />
      Your browser does not support WAV files in the audio element.
    </audio>
    <audio id="crash">
      <source src="../sounds/crash-trimmed.wav" type="audio/wav" />
      Your browser does not support WAV files in the audio element.
    </audio>

</body>
</html>
```

Example 8-11. JavaScript source for racing game engine

```
// Constructor
RacingGame = function()
{
    Sim.App.call(this);
}

// Subclass Sim.App
RacingGame.prototype = new Sim.App();
```

```javascript
// Our custom initializer
RacingGame.prototype.init = function(param)
{
    // Call superclass init code to set up scene, renderer,
    default camera
    Sim.App.prototype.init.call(this, param);

    param = param || {};
    this.param = param;

    this.hud = param.hud;
    this.sounds = param.sounds;

    this.createEnvironment();
    this.loadCars();
    this.loadRacer();

    this.curTime = Date.now();
    this.deltat = 0;

    this.running = false;
    this.state = RacingGame.STATE_LOADING;

    // Make sure the game has keyboard focus
    this.focus();

    this.addContextListener();
}

RacingGame.prototype.createEnvironment = function()
{
    this.environment = new Environment();
    this.environment.init({app:this,
        textureSky:true,
        textureGround:true,
        textureFinishLine:true,
        displaySigns:true});
    this.addObject(this.environment);
}

RacingGame.prototype.loadCars = function()
{
    this.carModels = [];
    this.nMakesLoaded = 0;
    this.nMakesTotal = 3;

    var that = this;
    var model = new JSONModel;
    model.init(
            {
                url : "../models/Nova Car/NovaCar.js",
                callback: function(model)
```

```
                            { that.onCarLoaded(model, "nova",
                            {
                                scale:0.7,
                                position:{x:0, y:.1, z:Car.CAR_LENGTH},
                                rotation:{x:-Math.PI / 2, y:0, z:0},
                            }); }
                    }
                    );

        model = new JSONModel;
        model.init(
                {
                    url : "../models/Camaro-1/Camaro.js",
                    callback: function(model)
                    { that.onCarLoaded(model, "camaro",
                    {
                        scale:0.17,
                        position:{x:1, y:-.5, z:Car.CAR_LENGTH},
                        rotation:{x:-Math.PI / 2, y:0, z:0},
                    }); }
                }
                );

        model = new JSONModel;
        model.init(
                {
                    url : "../models/Camaro-1/Camaro.js",
                    callback: function(model)
                    { that.onCarLoaded(model, "camaro_silver",
                    {
                        scale:0.17,
                        position:{x:1, y:-.5, z:Car.CAR_LENGTH},
                        rotation:{x:-Math.PI / 2, y:0, z:0},
                        map:"../models/Camaro-1/camaro_4.jpg",
                        mapIndex:0
                    }); }
                }
                );

}


RacingGame.prototype.onCarLoaded = function(model, make, options)
{
    this.carModels[this.nMakesLoaded++] =
        { make: make, model : model, options : options };

    if (this.nMakesLoaded >= this.nMakesTotal)
    {
        this.createCars();
    }
}
```

```
RacingGame.prototype.loadRacer = function()
{
    var that = this;
    var model = new JSONModel;
    model.init(
        { url : "../models/Nissan GTR OBJ/Objects/NissanOBJ1.js",
        scale:0.0254,
        callback: function(model) { that.onRacerLoaded(model); }
    });
}

RacingGame.prototype.onRacerLoaded = function(model)
{
    // Turn away from camera
    model.mesh.rotation.y = Math.PI;

    this.player = new Player;
    this.player.init(
        { mesh : model.object3D, camera : camera, exhaust:true,
        sounds : this.sounds});
    this.addObject(this.player);
    this.player.setPosition(0, RacingGame.CAR_Y + Environment.GROUND_Y,
            Environment.ROAD_LENGTH / 2 - RacingGame.PLAYER_START_Z);
    this.player.start();

    if (this.cars)
    {
        this.startGame();
    }
}

RacingGame.prototype.startGame = function()
{
    this.running = true;
    this.state = RacingGame.STATE_RUNNING;
    this.startTime = Date.now();

    if (this.sounds)
    {
        var driving = this.sounds["driving"];
        driving.loop = true;
        driving.play();
    }
}

RacingGame.prototype.finishGame = function()
{
    this.running = false;
    this.player.stop();

    var i, len = this.cars.length;
```

```
    for (i = 0; i < len; i++)
    {
        this.cars[i].stop();
    }

    this.state = RacingGame.STATE_COMPLETE;
    this.showResults();
}

RacingGame.prototype.crash = function(car)
{
    this.player.crash();
    car.crash();
    this.running = false;
    this.state = RacingGame.STATE_CRASHED;
    this.showResults();
}

RacingGame.prototype.createCars = function()
{
    this.cars = [];

    var i = 0, nCars = 5;
    for (i = 0; i < nCars; i++)
    {
        var object = this.createCar(i % this.nMakesLoaded);

        var car = new Car;
        car.init({ mesh : object });
        this.addObject(car);
        var randx = (Math.random() -.5 ) *
            (Environment.ROAD_WIDTH - Car.CAR_WIDTH);
        var randz = (Math.random()) *
            Environment.ROAD_LENGTH / 2 - RacingGame.CAR_START_Z;
        car.setPosition(randx, RacingGame.CAR_Y +
            Environment.GROUND_Y, randz);

        this.cars.push(car);
        car.start();
    }

    if (this.player)
    {
        this.startGame();
    }
}

RacingGame.prototype.createCar = function(makeIndex)
{
    var model = this.carModels[makeIndex].model;
    var options = this.carModels[makeIndex].options;
```

```
    var group = new THREE.Object3D;
    group.rotation.y = Math.PI;

    var mesh = new THREE.Mesh(model.mesh.geometry, model.mesh.material);
    mesh.rotation.set(options.rotation.x, options.rotation.y,
        options.rotation.z)
    mesh.scale.set(options.scale, options.scale, options.scale);
    mesh.position.set(options.position.x, options.position.y,
        options.position.z);

    if (options.map)
    {
        var material = mesh.geometry.materials[options.mapIndex];
        material.map = THREE.ImageUtils.loadTexture(options.map);
    }

    group.add(mesh);

    return group;
}

RacingGame.prototype.update = function()
{
    if (this.running)
    {
        this.elapsedTime = (Date.now() - this.startTime) / 1000;
        this.updateHUD();

        this.testCollision();

        if (this.player.object3D.position.z <
            (-Environment.ROAD_LENGTH / 2 - Car.CAR_LENGTH))
        {
            this.finishGame();
        }
    }

    Sim.App.prototype.update.call(this);
}

RacingGame.prototype.updateHUD = function()
{
    if (this.hud)
    {
        var kmh = this.player.speed * 3.6;   // convert m/s to km/hr
        this.hud.speedometer.update(kmh);

        this.hud.tachometer.update(this.player.rpm);

        this.hud.timer.innerHTML = "TIME<br>" +
            this.elapsedTime.toFixed(2);
```

```
            var roadRelative = (this.player.object3D.position.z -
                (Environment.ROAD_LENGTH / 2) + 4);
            var distanceKm = -roadRelative / Environment.ROAD_LENGTH;
            this.hud.odometer.innerHTML = "TRIP<br>" + distanceKm.toFixed(2);
    }
}

RacingGame.prototype.testCollision = function()
{
    var playerpos = this.player.object3D.position;

    if (playerpos.x > (Environment.ROAD_WIDTH / 2 - (Car.CAR_WIDTH/2)))
    {
        this.player.bounce();
        this.player.object3D.position.x -= 1;
    }

    if (playerpos.x < -(Environment.ROAD_WIDTH / 2 - (Car.CAR_WIDTH/2)))
    {
        this.player.bounce();
        this.player.object3D.position.x += 1;
    }

    var i, len = this.cars.length;
    for (i = 0; i < len; i++)
    {
        var carpos = this.cars[i].object3D.position;
        var dist = playerpos.distanceTo(carpos);
        if (dist < RacingGame.COLLIDE_RADIUS)
        {
            this.crash(this.cars[i]);
            break;
        }
    }
}

RacingGame.prototype.showResults = function()
{
    var overlay = document.getElementById("overlay");

    var headerHtml = "?";
    var contentsHtml = "?";
    var elapsedTime = this.elapsedTime.toFixed(2);

    if (this.state == RacingGame.STATE_COMPLETE)
    {
        if (elapsedTime < RacingGame.best_time)
        {
            RacingGame.best_time = elapsedTime;
        }

        headerHtml = "RACE COMPLETE!";
```

```
            contentsHtml =
                "ELAPSED TIME: " + elapsedTime +
                "s<p>BEST TIME: " + RacingGame.best_time + "s";

    }
    else if (this.state == RacingGame.STATE_CRASHED)
    {
        headerHtml = "CRASHED!";
        contentsHtml =
            "CRASH TIME: " + elapsedTime + "s";
    }

    var header = document.getElementById("header");
    var contents = document.getElementById("contents");
    header.innerHTML = headerHtml;
    contents.innerHTML = contentsHtml;

    overlay.style.display = "block";
}


RacingGame.prototype.handleKeyDown = function(keyCode, charCode)
{
    if (this.player)
    {
        this.player.handleKeyDown(keyCode, charCode);
    }
}

RacingGame.prototype.handleKeyUp = function(keyCode, charCode)
{
    if (this.player)
    {
        this.player.handleKeyUp(keyCode, charCode);
    }
}

RacingGame.prototype.restart = function(e)
{
    // Re-init the sounds
    if (this.sounds)
    {
        var driving = this.sounds["driving"];
        driving.pause();
        driving.currentTime = 0;
    }

    // Hide the overlay
    var overlay = document.getElementById("overlay");
    overlay.style.display = 'none';

    // Reinitialize us
```

```
        this.container.removeChild(this.renderer.domElement);
        this.init( this.param );
    }

    RacingGame.prototype.handleContextLost = function(e)
    {
        this.restart();
    }

    RacingGame.prototype.addContextListener = function()
    {
        var that = this;

        this.renderer.domElement.addEventListener("webglcontextlost",
                function(e) {
                    that.handleContextLost(e);
                    },
                false);
    }

    RacingGame.COLLIDE_RADIUS = Math.sqrt(2 * Car.CAR_WIDTH);
    RacingGame.STATE_LOADING = 0;
    RacingGame.STATE_RUNNING = 1;
    RacingGame.STATE_COMPLETE = 2;
    RacingGame.STATE_CRASHED = 3;
    RacingGame.CAR_Y = .4666;
    RacingGame.CAR_START_Z = 10;
    RacingGame.PLAYER_START_Z = 4;
    RacingGame.best_time = Number.MAX_VALUE;
```

Chapter Summary

So that's how we build a game in WebGL. I know it was a simple game, a bit contrived
for teaching purposes. Still, it has all the elements of real games you would create using
WebGL. It took me about four days to write, including wrangling all the content. Admittedly, I was building upon the great foundation of Three.js, as well as my modest
Sim.js framework—and that made a lot of the going easy. Still, it is a testament to the
power of WebGL, the browser as application platform, and the free and open nature of
HTML5 that I was able to put this together so quickly.

In this chapter, we reviewed the main topics of the book, including graphics, animation,
interaction, and 2D/3D integration. We got a deeper look into production issues and
revisited building robust applications. We also learned a few new tricks, like how to
create a cool special effect and incorporate sound. Folks, we've now hit cruising speed;
the only thing left to talk about is where we go from here.

Afterword

So, where do we go from here? We've seen what it takes to build a WebGL application. It's not the easiest thing in the world, but now that we've been through it, I think you would agree that it's not rocket science either. Sure, there are some new concepts—even a few downright foreign ideas in there—but nothing we can't tackle with a little practice.

By now I hope you can imagine developing a production site with WebGL and how it will fit into your infrastructure, as well as how to tune it to meet your own needs. This book covered several topics you will inevitably touch upon in your projects—WebGL API concepts, 3D graphics programming, the Three.js toolkit, and content creation, to name a few—but these are just the tip of a deep iceberg. The feature set is so powerful, and the possibilities so vast, that there is still much to learn on the road ahead.

WebGL has moved from the infant stage into toddlerhood; it has a lot of growing up to do, but we can clearly see outlines of the adult that it will one day become. The standard is well thought out and thoroughly vetted, but the ink is only just dry; the first browsers shipped with the final version 1 specification just over a year ago. In my experience, the implementations have been rock-solid. I tested the examples in Chrome, Firefox, and Safari; they all looked great and performed well, and most importantly, they worked identically across the browsers. The tools are still mishmash and need a lot of work, but they will get there. Thanks to open source, a global development community, and blazingly fast JavaScript virtual machines, there is no telling what kind of great tools we'll see in the coming months.

Three.js is my favorite library, but it's not the whole universe when it comes to coding in WebGL. Alexander Rodic's amazing jellyfish forest wasn't built with Three.js; neither was Google's incredible human body simulation. Take a look at the other toolkits. You may find another runtime that you like more, or that fits the application requirements better. Or you may get inspired to write an engine yourself. I've made no secret of my opinion that the WebGL API was not designed for mere mortals; but perhaps you're one of those demigods who can think in buffers and matrices all day long. If that's the case, I look forward to taking your engine for a spin someday.

The places we can take WebGL are virtually limitless. In this book, we barely scratched the surface on graphics. We stuck to the basics and, in the interests of ramping up fast, remained aloof regarding programmable shaders. It's too bad, because that's where most of the raw power lies. On the other hand, shaders are a bit of a powder keg. Now that you have a firm grounding in the fundamentals of 3D application development, it probably makes sense to go write a shader or two—if for no other reason than to be able to say you did. We also breezed through topics ranging from information design to game development, disciplines that are going to get a fresh infusion of energy from readers like yourself, using the world as your WebGL development sandbox.

WebGL is a canvas: paint it with broad strokes or fine, push it, pull it, and shape it to your needs. WebGL is a tool: leverage it to extract maximum value. WebGL is a new medium, with new rules and responsibilities: take care and use as directed. Most important, WebGL is 3D in your browser, right here, right now. No more future promises; we have arrived.

WebGL Resources

If you type "WebGL" into your favorite search engine, you will find no shortage of hits. However, the key is to get the information that is relevant for you. This appendix compiles a categorized list of my favorite sites. I frequent many of them to find the latest technical information, cutting-edge demos, and thought pieces by the leaders in the community. Happy hunting!

The WebGL Specification

The WebGL standard is developed and maintained by the Khronos Group, the industry body that also governs OpenGL, COLLADA, and other specifications you may have heard of. You can always find the latest version of the official WebGL specification on the Khronos website at *http://www.khronos.org/registry/webgl/specs/latest/*.

Official Mailing Lists and Forums

Khronos maintains a public mailing list to discuss drafts of the WebGL specification. You can subscribe to the list, *public_webgl@khronos.org*, by following the instructions at *http://www.khronos.org/webgl/public-mailing-list/*.

There is also a Google group for discussing more general WebGL development topics outside of the core specification. You can sign up for this list at *https://groups.google.com/forum/?fromgroups#!forum/webgl-dev-list*.

Tools and Toolkits

The past few years have seen the emergence of several libraries and tools for use with WebGL. Here is a list of some good ones, in no particular order. Some are open source; some are proprietary and may come with licensing restrictions.

Three.js (https://github.com/mrdoob/three.js/)

An open source JavaScript 3D engine; the library used for most of the examples in this book. Three.js provides an easy, intuitive set of objects that are commonly found in 3D graphics. Three.js is maintained by a strong team of contributors.

GLGE (http://www.glge.org/)

An open source JavaScript library intended to ease the use and minimize the setup time of WebGL so that developers can then spend their time creating richer content for the Web.

SceneJS (http://www.scenejs.org/)

An open source 3D engine for JavaScript that provides a JSON-based scene graph API on WebGL. SceneJS specializes in efficient rendering of large numbers of individually pickable and articulated objects as required by high-detail model-viewing applications in engineering and medicine.

CubicVR (http://www.cubicvr.org/)

A high-performance object-oriented OpenGL 2.0 and OpenGL ES 3D engine, recently ported from C++ to JavaScript. It is used by Mozilla Labs as the basis for its WebGL projects and its Gladius game engine, a part of the Paladin open source game technology initiative (*https://wiki.mozilla.org/Paladin*).

KickJS (http://www.kickjs.org/)

An open source game engine built for WebGL. KickJS has a rich feature set for rendering, interaction, serialization, and game behaviors.

CopperLicht (http://www.ambiera.com/copperlicht/)

A "Commercial grade WebGL 3D engine with editor," according to the website. CopperLicht is free to use, and there are commercial licenses available that provide access to uncompressed, documented source and customer support.

Sunglass (http://sunglass.io/)

More of a collaborative design product than a toolkit, with an innovative WebGL frontend that allows designers to build together.

Sim.js (https://github.com/tparisi/Sim.js)

A simple simulation framework for WebGL. This is my open source project that attempts to wrap the more repetitive Three.js tasks, such as setup and teardown, the run loop, and DOM event handling, into a small set of easy-to-use JavaScript classes. Sim.js is good for small projects but probably too simplistic for large-scale WebGL development.

Blogs and Demo Sites

Most likely, your main source of fresh, up-to-the-minute practical information on WebGL will come from one of the many fantastic blog sites devoted to the topic. Here are some that I visit on a regular basis:

Learning WebGL (http://learningwebgl.com/blog/)
> The granddaddy of WebGL sites, written by Giles Thomas. This should be your very first stop to learn the basics of low-level WebGL programming and use of the API.

WebGL Fundamentals (http://games.greggman.com/game/webgl-fundamentals/)
> Written by Gregg Tavares, one of the main WebGL developers on the Google Chrome team.

Learning Three.js (http://learningthreejs.com/)
> The blog site of Jerome Etienne, focused on Three.js and hands-on development topics.

Three.js on Reddit (http://www.reddit.com/r/threejs)
> A Reddit for Three.js, maintained by Theo Armour and updated frequently. This Reddit is a grab bag of demos, techniques, news, and articles.

WebGL.com
> Curated by New York-based Darien Acosta. This is a site for discovering new WebGL games, demos, and applications.

WebGL Mozilla Labs Demos (https://developer.mozilla.org/en-US/demos/tag/tech:webgl/)
> Demos created by Mozilla Labs and partners.

WebGL Chrome Experiments (http://www.chromeexperiments.com/webgl)
> Demos created by Google and partners.

Community Sites

I host a WebGL Meetup group for the Bay Area (*http://www.meetup.com/WebGL-Developers-Meetup/*). Meetups are a great way to get together with like-minded individuals. If you don't live around here, search Meetups.com for a WebGL group in your area, or start one yourself!

You can also find a great community in the WebGL LinkedIn group (*http://www.linkedin.com/groups/WebGL-3724416*) and the Facebook page (*http://www.facebook.com/pages/WebGL/109400139085505*).

Index

We'd like to hear your suggestions for improving our indexes. Send email to index@oreilly.com.

About the Author

Tony Parisi is an entrepreneur and career CTO/architect. He has developed international standards and protocols, created noteworthy software products, and started and sold technology companies. Tony's passion for innovating is exceeded only by his desire to bring coolness and fun to the broadest possible audience.

Tony is perhaps best known for his work as a pioneer of 3D standards for the web. He is the cocreator of VRML and X3D, ISO standards for networked 3D graphics. He also codeveloped SWMP, a real-time messaging protocol for multiuser virtual worlds. Tony continues to build community around innovations in 3D as the cochair of the WebGL Meetup and a founder of the Rest3D working group.

Tony is currently a partner in a stealth online gaming startup and has a consulting practice developing social games, virtual worlds and location-based services for San Francisco Bay Area clients.

Colophon

The animal on the cover of *WebGL: Up and Running* is a chrysaora. A genus of marine jellyfish from the Scyphozoa class, chrysaora are found all over the world in both tropical and temperate inshore waters. There are several species of chrysaora, and a common one is known as the Pacific sea nettle. This variety of jellyfish are typically found along the coasts of Oregon and California. The word "chrysaora" stems from Greek mythology; Chrysaor was the son of Poseidon and Medusa, and brother of Pegasus. When translated, it means "he who has a golden armament."

Chrysaora are elegant creatures, and are noted for their long, thin tentacles—about 24 in total—attached to an opaque bell. The bell carries pulsations that help chrysaora, using a form of jet propulsion, travel through water. Their tentacles can grow more than three feet in length, depending on the species, and are used to catch the planktonic animals they eat. While humans fear a chrysaora's sting, it is only deadly to small prey. Chrysaora are also hermaphrodites, reproducing asexually, and the average lifespan for a chrysaora is about one year. Additionally, species vary greatly in color and size, which makes them popular for aquarium exhibits.

There is in fact a direct association between WebGL development and the chrysaora. Chrysaora.com features a demo of WebGL, simulating jellyfish pulsating underwater—in real-time—rendered in 3D. The demo was created by Aleksandar Rodic, and utilizes numerous programming languages, including JavaScript, CSS, and Python. Site visitors can tweak the simulation, controlling shadows, speed, and even the number of jellyfish in the rendering itself.

The cover image is from *Beauties of Land and Sea*. The cover font is Adobe ITC Garamond. The text font is Minion Pro by Robert Slimbach; the heading font is Myriad Pro by Robert Slimbach and Carol Twombly; and the code font is UbuntuMono by Dalton Maag.

Have it your way.

Ingram Content Group UK Ltd.
Milton Keynes UK
UKHW031934110423
419994UK00010B/915